Berlitz®

Vancouver

Original text by Paula Tevis
Updated by Jack Christie
Series Editor: Tony Halliday

Berlitz POCKET GUIDE

Vancouver

Third Edition 2005

PHOTOGRAPHY
Apa 6, 12, 61, 69, 74; City of Vancouver Archives 16; Jackie Garrow 73, 83; Richard Nowitz/1, 9, 10, 19, 21, 22, 24, 28, 30/1, 33, 36, 38, 39, 40, 42, 46, 53, 55, 56, 65, 66, 70, 79, 85, 87, 91, 94, 98, 100; Doug Plummer 13, 25, 27, 41, 47, 48, 52, 60, 64, 96, 102; Joel W. Rogers 35, 43, 45, 51, 59, 63, 76, 86, 88, 92; Stanley Young/City of Vancouver Archives 18; Stanley Young/Vancouver Public Library 15.
Cover photograph: Stuart Dee/The Image Bank/Getty Images

CONTACTING THE EDITORS
Every effort has been made to provide accurate information in this publication, but changes are inevitable. The publisher cannot be responsible for any resulting loss, inconvenience or injury. We would appreciate it if readers would call our attention to any errors or outdated information by contacting Berlitz Publishing, PO Box 7910, London SE1 1WE, England. Fax: (44) 20 7403 0290; e-mail: berlitz@apaguide.co.uk www.berlitzpublishing.com

Stanley Park (page 27) is a verdant oasis at the heart of the city. Walk the seawall promenade, shown here

The Vancouver Aquarium (page 30) is one of the best of its kind in North America

The Museum of Anthropology (page 50) is home to a splendid collection of First Nations artefacts

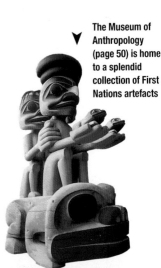

TOP TEN ATTRACTIONS

TELUSphere (page 44) is a multi-level, heavily interactive science museum

For authentic Chinese markets, shops, gardens and restaurants, visit the engaging Chinatown (page 41)

Vancouver Museum (page 46) guides visitors through several thousand years of local history

The busy Waterfront (page 33) is dominated by these five distinctive white sails

Historic Gastown (page 39) is now a commercial district

Broad, leafy Robson Square (page 35) is a great place to take a break

Granville Island (page 42) bristles with markets, restaurants, museums and artists' studios

CONTENTS

Introduction 7

A Brief History 13

Where to Go 25

A ➤ in the text denotes a highly recommended sight

Stanley Park and the West End 27
  Stanley Park 27, West End and Denman Street 32

Downtown Vancouver 33
  The Waterfront 34, Robson Street and the Central
  Business District 35, Hornby to Burrard 36, Gastown 38,
  Chinatown 40

False Creek and Granville Island 42
  Granville Island 42, Yaletown 44

The West Side and The East Side 45
  Kitsilano 45, Vanier Park and Vancouver Museum 46,
  Maritime Museum 47, Pioneer Park and Jericho
  Beach 48, Point Grey and the University of B.C. 49,
  Shaughnessy and Little Mountain 52, The East Side:
  Commercial Drive 54

Excursions 54
  North Vancouver 54, West Vancouver 59, Bowen Island 61,
  Whistler 63, Steveston 66, Vancouver Island and Victoria 68

What to Do 77

Entertainment and Nightlife 77

Shopping 82

Sports 86

Children 90

Eating Out 94

Handy Travel Tips 103

Hotels and Restaurants 126

Recommended Hotels 126, Recommended Restaurants 135

Index 143

Fact Sheets

Historical Landmarks 23
Plaques and Statues 26
Moshe Safdie 37
First Nations 50
Howe Sound Activities 62
The Scandalous Mr Rattenbury 71
Vancouver Goes to the Movies 81
Vancouver Children's Festival 90
Festivals and Events 93
Wild About Salmon 97

INTRODUCTION

Imagine for a moment that you are on a broad walkway that winds along a boat-filled harbour. As you relax on a smooth wooden bench, your eyes rest on a great swath of forest a stone's throw away. An endless stretch of mountains, woolly with trees, provides the background a few kilometres north, beckoning past the dark blue waters of the inlet that divides the shores. Behind you, the late afternoon sun has transformed a dozen glass high-rises into glistening emerald-, ruby-, and sapphire-toned baubles. Now turn east along the bay, catching sight of five enormous white sails that majestically anchor the tip of downtown, and the next thing you know, you are completely infatuated with Vancouver.

The Best of Both Worlds

Canada's third-largest city is a visual delight no matter where you linger, but it's more than just a pretty face. Vancouver works hard to maximise the beauty of its surroundings. Multi-storey office, condominium and apartment buildings dominate the skyline, yet their occupants nearly always enjoy a view of the mountains or sea from a multitude of windows and the requisite balcony. On busy downtown streets, merely walk a block or so – or simply turn your head – and you'll be treated to the sight of the Coast Mountains, the splendours of Stanley Park, the waters of Burrard Inlet, or all three if you're particularly well situated. Notice, too, what isn't there. Rubbish, for instance. Here you have an urban, densely populated, popular destination and it's clean. Even the air smells delicious, due in part to the lack of downtown freeways. While there is no shortage of cars, the powers-that-be bowed to the

West Coast First Nations are famed for their wood-carving skills

demands of an occasionally vocal majority and eschewed mazes of concrete for clear vistas. An efficient choice? Perhaps not. A thoughtful and appropriate one? Certainly.

Rather than encourage even more vehicles by building those freeways, city planners for the Greater Vancouver Regional District implemented ideas for mixed-use zoning and modest transport options that would lead to several sophisticated commercial areas rather than just the one. Vancouver itself deliberately re-zoned city-centre land for residential use, resulting over the years in the development of vibrant neighbourhoods as exemplified by the West End, Yaletown and False Creek. The result is a compact, easy-to-absorb, simple-to-navigate, open and accessible city that is conscious of its charms and careful to preserve them.

Foresight and Imagination

Mistakes were made, naturally, such as the demolition in the 1960s of older single-family homes in the West End to make way for unattractive litters of apartment towers, but for the most part the city recognises its treasures. This can sometimes be credited to foresight. Stanley Park must surely have started the blood rushing through many an ambitious developer in the early days, yet the original city council's first vote was to lease these 405 hectares (1,000 acres) from the federal government for a park. Sometimes it can be traced to imagination. Granville Island was little more than an industrial wasteland after World War II, until a group of politicians and business-people in the early 1970s envisaged it for public use and created one of the most popular destinations in the entire city for both locals and tourists.

In other cases, these decisions are due to a confluence of luck and timing. Pacific Spirit Park, part of the university's endowment lands, was saved from becoming a housing tract through a combination of unfortunate circumstances (unfor-

Canada Place and the cruise ship terminal

tunate for the would-be developers, that is) and community activism. Vancouverites may claim to be politically apathetic, but they know when to rally round a good cause.

Cultural Diversity

The city's half-million residents (with another 1.9 million in the Greater Vancouver metropolitan area) represent an amalgam of cultures from Europe, Asia, Latin America and British Columbia's indigenous population. Fully 50 percent of Greater Vancouver residents are Asian. After English, Mandarin Chinese is the language most often spoken. The treatment by the early ruling class of many ethnic groups (particularly the Chinese prior to 1947, the Japanese at the turn of the century and during World War II and the Sikhs in 1914) left much to be desired, but over the years Vancouver has evolved. The city is considered not only a bastion for tolerance and acceptance, but a model. And despite the multi-

The renovated Sinclair Building

culturalism – or more likely because of it – some delightful, all-pervasive local ethic provides the tie that binds. Vancouverites, no matter from whence they hail, bear a well-deserved reputation for being friendly, polite and open-minded. They are also rather modest, often crediting their fine traits as being somehow 'Canadian' in nature.

Outdoor Life

A second principle the locals live by involves being outdoors as often as possible. Vancouverites work hard, but they play harder, tackling their days off with all the exuberance of school kids let out at break time. Walking, running, hiking, in-line skating, swimming, kayaking, sailing, skiing – when sports-obsessed citizens flip open the mobile phone, chances are they are setting up a jogging date, not a meeting. And the weather is no excuse to cancel. Folks here don't change their plans because of rain, even with a yearly average of 170 days of drizzle. A reputation for wet weather notwithstanding, Vancouver has the mildest climate of any Canadian city. This is one reason why so many residents have moved here from other parts of the nation.

Along with its good-natured citizenry and glorious location, the city's appeal also lies in the fact that it retains a small-town sensibility despite its status as a major port and trading partner in the Pacific Rim. The engaging neighbourhoods, from trendy Yaletown to the more traditional Point Grey, can each be accurately characterised in a sentence, and you can visit them all in a day, practically on foot. Drivers stop (not just slow down) for pedestrians, and they take turns merging on the Lions Gate Bridge during rush hour. Since you can't really tell the tourists from the locals, if you drop by the same coffee bar two mornings in a row, you'll be considered a regular.

A Seamier Side

In reality, though, Vancouver is a big city, and like all big cities it has an underbelly. Vancouver's importance as a world port is both a blessing and a bit of a curse. Alaskan cruise ships make regular use of Vancouver's berths, every year contributing over $300 million to the economy and setting down over 800,000 passengers for a day or more of shopping and sightseeing. Container shipping is big business too, and billions of dollars-worth of goods pass through Vancouver on their way to Pacific Rim destinations.

Economic benefits aside, busy ports attract the drug trade, and Vancouver has been a hot spot for trafficking since opium users were a source of civic shame back at the turn of the 20th century. A century later they've been replaced by cocaine and heroin addicts, who the city attempts to control by corralling them inside the downtown East Side. Canada's sane gun-control laws help to keep major crime in check, however. Vehicle break-ins are actually the most common aggravation anyone faces in Vancouver, and it's a problem that is easily solved by keeping the car's interior devoid of anything worth pawning.

> **There are lots of jokes about B.C. weather, with the state dubbed 'The Wet Coast'. The locals take this in their stride and joke about it. 'You don't tan in Vancouver,' they say. 'You rust.'**

Mountains frame many city views

Engaging in controversy over the drug issue (or anything else, for that matter) isn't a popular pastime here, and the city atmosphere is terminally laid-back. If New York is suits and attitude, and L.A. is sunglasses and tummy tucks, Vancouver is, well, cargo pants and polar fleece (or shorts and sandals, depending on the weather). No one is too hurried to give directions, admonitions to walk your bike on certain parts of the seawall are gentle, and there's no attitude in the fancy restaurants. As one local put it, 'we're just into living'.

Simply the Best

They must be onto something. In 2005, Vancouver was ranked third out of 215 cities worldwide for best places to live in the annual quality of life survey by Mercer Human Resource Consulting, and was voted 'Best City in the Americas' by *Condé Nast Traveller* readers. Along with the accolades come more and more tourists – 8.5 million per year at last count – and Vancouver continues to work on the infrastructure to accommodate them, including hotels, a new conference centre, and another cruise ship terminal. Little of this crosses one's mind, however, when sitting on the sand overlooking English Bay, with the sun drifting into the sea. The overwhelming beauty is all you really need to know about Vancouver.

A BRIEF HISTORY

A dependable supply of salmon, shellfish and plant life provided the west coast First Nations with plenty of food. This bounty, together with milder winters than their prairie counterparts had to endure, allowed them the leisure to hone sophisticated skills such as wood carving and to develop an advanced culture that included ceremonial customs to celebrate marriages, births and alliances. One such practice was the *potlatch*, in which entire tribes would be entertained lavishly at gatherings planned years in advance. Such a ceremony aided in transmitting news and stories to attendees and conferred great status on the hosts.

It is not known precisely how many Coast Salish people lived in the area that was to become Vancouver, but smallpox epidemics are blamed for decimating a majority of the population in the 1700s and early 1800s. Those who survived encountered a small but steady stream of explorers, beginning with the Spaniard José María Navarez in 1791. He was quickly followed by Captain George Vancouver in 1792. Representing Great Britain, Vancouver arrived with the two-fold intention of mapping the Northwest Coast and negotiating with Navarez's successor, Juan Francisco de la Bodega y Quadra, regarding a dispute involving Spain's capture of three British ships in 1789. Vancouver spent three consecutive summers surveying the coast, naming over 400

Totem poles, Vancouver

places, including Vancouver Island (he originally called it 'Quadra and Vancouver Island', to commemorate his friendly relationship with the rival captain). It would be another 90 years before the developing city on the mainland would bear his name as well.

Fur, Fish and Gold

Fur trading brought the first group of English settlers to the Greater Vancouver area in 1827. They were employees of the Hudson's Bay Company, and they built Fort Langley on the Fraser River, approximately 50km (31 miles) from today's Vancouver. The lucrative fur trade was equalled and soon surpassed by salmon exports in the 1840s, when Fort Langley was the largest exporter of fish on the Pacific Coast.

Despite these early commercial successes, it was the 1858 announcement that gold had been discovered in the Fraser River that spurred the British, who were already governing Vancouver Island (calling it 'British Columbia'), to declare the mainland a colony as well. They did so in response to the 25,000-plus gold diggers from the United States who converged on the river, still seeking the riches that had eluded them back in California during the Gold Rush of 1849.

Though hordes of prospectors were making their way through the largely unsettled mainland, the European population around Burrard Inlet was still almost non-existent. To encourage growth, the governor of Vancouver Island, James Douglas, initiated a law allowing Europeans to appropriate land not settled by First Nations, who, as fate would have it, had defined but small, summer and winter settlements.

Timber was the first big money-spinner for B.C., with reserves around Burrard Inlet set aside to supply masts for ships of the Royal Navy, and other exports going to Australia.

Gigantic trees brought prosperity to British Columbia's sawmills

Birth of the City

This encouraged three English prospectors to clear a plot of land near what is now the West End of the city. Vancouver was finally off to a start, if not a particularly rousing one.

In 1867, the first mill on the south shore opened just blocks from the heart of today's Gastown at the end of Dunlevy Street. Originally named after its owner, Edward Stamp, it later became Hastings Mill; the village around it took the name Hastings Township. That same year, Canada officially became a country and John Deighton paddled into Burrard Inlet with a small entourage and a keg of whisky. At the time, the closest bar was an inconvenient half day's walk away. 'Gassy Jack', as the garrulous Deighton became known, was persuasive enough – or the mill workers were thirsty enough – to convince the settlers to build him a saloon within 24 hours of his arrival, and Gastown, as the settlement was soon nicknamed, was on the map.

Vancouver's large Asian community has historic origins

The Railway Arrives

While the land closer to the Fraser River was peopled with farmers and fishermen, there wasn't much to Gastown (officially known as 'Granville') outside of 'Gassy' Jack's hotel-saloon, 22 other saloons, the brothels, the mill and a few stores and houses. This was all poised to change in 1871, when the province of British Columbia linked its fate with the young country of Canada and joined the Confederation. B.C.'s provincial government did so on a promise from the powerful Canadian Pacific Railway (CPR) to extend its reach into the hinterlands. A second promise by the government to gift the CPR 2,428 hectares (6,000 acres) on Burrard Peninsula sealed the deal to make Granville the railway's west-coast terminus.

The CPR's general manager, William Van Horne, is credited with renaming scruffy Granville 'Vancouver', in his opinion a much grander name that was more in keeping with the town's future. Vancouver was incorporated in 1886, its city councillors were elected, and their initial piece of business resulted in the acquisition of a lease for a military reserve that they wanted to develop as a park – Stanley Park, in fact.

Rising From the Ashes

Two months after its incorporation, Vancouver, with its new name, its new city government, and its new status as the end of the transcontinental railway line, was destroyed by a rogue fire. Undaunted, the city started its new life by reconstruction from scratch, replacing the ramshackle wooden buildings with fine new brick ones befitting its status.

Chinatown

Of all the immigrants flooding into Vancouver, the Chinese had a particularly difficult time, as targets of severe racism. As early as 1858, they migrated from San Francisco seeking gold, and their numbers increased dramatically between 1881 and 1885, drawn by jobs on the railway. They suffered humiliation from discriminatory laws that prevented them from working on government-financed projects, levied a head tax, and eventually prohibited immigration. In 1907, anti-Chinese riots caused massive destruction in Chinatown.

Yet the Chinese community persevered. They formed 'benevolent societies' to assist one another and fight the unfair laws. Finally, the 1923 Chinese Immigration Act was repealed in 1947 and eventually Vancouver's Chinatown became the largest in Canada and the third largest in North America. More recently, wealthy Hong Kong Chinese relocated here prior to the repossession of Hong Kong by China in 1997, building elaborate homes and investing money in real estate and other businesses. Some have since returned to their homeland, but Asians now make up 50 percent of the population and have produced a new generation of business and civic leaders.

Vancouver in the 20th Century

The somewhat sedate and well-ordered Vancouver of the new millennium is quite a contrast to the rough-and-tumble town that quickly sprouted from the ashes of the great fire. From the beginning, Vancouver's explosive growth was accompanied by less-than-exemplary behaviour from a good many citizens. Prostitution, which had gained an early foothold in the economy, found bedfellows in gambling and opium dens, and Vancouverites were reported to imbibe more alcohol per capita than any other Canadians. But a semblance of sophistication also found its way into town: Sarah Bernhardt performed at the Vancouver Opera House in 1891; the Carnegie Library at Hastings and Main Streets was erected in 1903 (it's now a community centre); and the first skyscraper, the 13-storey Dominion Trust Building on Hastings and Cambie streets, went up in 1909.

Vancouver c.1930

By 1911, the suburbs surrounding Vancouver, including Richmond, South Vancouver, and Point Grey, were connected to the city centre by electric streetcars, which brought 100,000 passengers daily to work and shop.

World Wars and the Great Depression

With World War I came a reduction in trade and the end of the mining boom in the province, but the following decade brought new

The stylish art deco interior of the Marine Building

growth. The largest dance hall in B.C. was built on Bowen Island in 1921, and the University of British Columbia finally moved to its new Point Grey campus in 1925, 10 years after classes had first begun. Point Grey and South Vancouver merged with Vancouver in 1928, adding another 80,000 people to the roster and making Vancouver the third-largest city in Canada.

During the Great Depression of the 1930s, destitute people from all over the country migrated to Vancouver hoping to find work, but found there was little to be had. Despite the financial crash, progress crept along. A new city hall was built out in the 'sticks' at 12th and Cambie streets, the Vancouver Art Gallery opened, and the Lions Gate Bridge united West and North Vancouver and Stanley Park in 1938. The bridge was built, at a cost of almost $6 million, by the wealthy Guinness family to provide access to their new North Shore housing development.

During World War I, some 28,000 citizens of Vancouver joined the armed forces, the greatest number from any North American city. An equally impressive contribution was made to World War II, when the city's women stepped up in tens of thousands to run the city's shipyards, mills and businesses.

World War II curtailed the unemployment problem in Canada as it did in all of North America, but the bombing of Pearl Harbor, bringing Japan into the war, led to the internment of Japanese-Canadians – 9,000 of them from Vancouver alone – and the selling off of their homes for 10 cents on the dollar. This had an effect on the demographics of the village of Steveston, along the Fraser River, where many Japanese fishermen and cannery workers had lived and worked. A more hopeful note was sounded in 1947, when Chinese and East Indians were given the vote in provincial elections, followed in 1949 by the enfranchisement of both the Japanese and the First Nations populations.

The Post-War Period

As Vancouver settled into the calm of the post-war 1950s, the population began shifting from the city to the suburbs, with less than half of the 800,000-plus residents of the Greater Vancouver metropolitan area actually residing inside the city's limits. In recognition of the North Shore's growing influence, the first Canadian shopping mall was built, in well-to-do West Vancouver, and the Lions Gate Bridge changed from private to public ownership.

Hippies discovered the West Side neighbourhood of Kitsilano in the 1960s, and developers changed the face of the West End from a district of single family homes to a high-density enclave of apartment towers and condominiums. Local protests over a proposed downtown freeway muzzled a plan to cut through the East Side's Strathcona neighbourhood during this decade as well. Activism at the grassroots level progressed on other issues and precipitated the birth of the environmental group Greenpeace and the rebirth of the long-neglected Gastown district, the city's birthplace.

The One Million Mark

The 1971 census proclaimed that there were now a million residents in the Greater Vancouver region. Some of the city's most interesting and popular sites were built during this decade, such as the Museum of Anthropology, Granville Island, the VanDusen Botanical Garden, the Stanley Park seawall and the Steam Clock in Gastown. In 1978 Vancouver also launched the world's first festival specifically for children, one of many annual celebrations that continue to add to the vibrancy of the city.

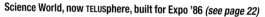

Science World, now TELUSphere, built for Expo '86 *(see page 22)*

The modern face of Vancouver

It took one event in particular, Expo '86, to catapult Vancouver into the international spotlight. Marking the city's 100th birthday, this world fair attracted over 22 million visitors from 44 countries, who dropped by for the 165-day celebration with the theme 'World in Motion, World in Touch'. Canada Place, with its trademark five white sails, Science World (now TELUSphere), and SkyTrain, the city's light-rail rapid transit system, were among the party favours dispensed by Expo. But its most enduring legacy was the raising of Vancouver's handsome profile on the world stage. The city hasn't been the same since.

Urban Revitalisation

During the 1980s and 1990s over 107,000 people moved into the downtown area, reversing a decades-long flow to the suburbs. This has given the city a particularly welcoming atmosphere as residents and visitors mingle on city streets long after businesses have finished for the day. To accommodate and even encourage this trend, new neighbourhoods are in the planning and construction stage as Vancouver prepares to host the 2010 Winter Olympic Games.

Trade with Asia, despite the recession, continues to grow apace, complemented by new markets that have opened up in South America and all over the extended city of just under 2 million residents, sustainable growth and opportunity continue to be the watchwords. After 120 years nothing, and everything, has changed.

Historical Landmarks

c.500BC Earliest settlement of Vancouver area by Northwest Coast people at Ee'yullmough Village, Jericho Beach.

AD 1791 Spaniard José María Navarez sails into Burrard Inlet.

1792 Captain George Vancouver, of the British Royal Navy, claims the region for the Crown.

1827 The Hudson's Bay Company establish a fur trading post, Fort Langley, on the south shore of the Fraser River.

1850 Smallpox decimates the First Nations population, decreasing their number from 150,000 to 60,000.

1851 Gold is discovered on the Fraser River drainage, attracting 22,000 prospectors, including the first Chinese settlers. Britain designates the territory the 'Colony of British Columbia'.

1864 First timber export departs for Australia. Governor Douglas creates First Nations reserves.

1867 Jack Deighton builds his saloon in the settlement that becomes known as 'Gastown'.

1884 Floating salmon canneries dump waste into Coal Harbour, causing fish to die – Vancouver's first pollution problem.

1886 'Gastown' is renamed twice: first Granville, then Vancouver.

1887 The Canadian Pacific's transcontinental railway line is completed.

1929 British Columbia has 4,000 logging operations and 350 mills.

1937 Students at a Strathcona school represent 57 nationalities.

1947–8 First Nations and Asian residents granted the vote.

1967 Environmental Group, Greenpeace, is founded in Vancouver.

1986 Expo '86 establishes Vancouver as an international trade and tourism destination.

1992 Vancouver-born Kim Campbell becomes British Columbia's first Prime Minister of Canada.

1999 Population of Vancouver approaches 2 million.

2002 Vancouver one of top three 'best cities in the world to live'.

2003 The city is chosen to host the 2010 Winter Olympic Games.

2004 Work begins on Olympic venues. Property prices boom again.

WHERE TO GO

Vancouver is composed of neighbourhoods with personalities so distinct that you really don't need a map to tell you when you've moved from one to another. It might be the slight shift in style that tips you off when, for example, South Granville's antiques shops give way to Kitsilano's kitchenware emporia, or perhaps a more obvious shift in cultures as you progress through the narrow aisles of Chinatown groceries towards Commercial Drive's coffee houses.

This juxtaposition of varied styles and cultures would be enough to make Vancouver an entertaining destination, but the city has the added bonus of an exquisite natural setting, almost surrounded by water, with majestic mountains as a backdrop. The land and the sea contribute so much of what makes the city immensely desirable that, even when you are confined inside four walls, the architecture makes the most of what lies beyond the windows or above the skylights.

Dragon at a Stanley Park festival

Walkability

Wherever you choose to go in Vancouver, it is likely that the outdoors will be an integral part of your plans. Ideally, you'll want to approach your destination wearing a comfortable pair of shoes, for, like all great cities, Vancouver is designed for exploration on foot. Urban planners have provided

The harbour at sunset

pedestrians with delightful roads to tread. A truly determined walker (or cyclist) could start on an approximately 22-km (13½-mile) path at Canada Place that eventually leads around Stanley Park and English Bay, circles False Creek, and ends at lovely Kitsilano Beach for a well-deserved, relaxing soak in the bay.

A more idyllic – and certainly less strenuous – day could begin with a stroll in one of Vancouver's downtown neighbourhoods such as Yaletown or the West End, Chinatown or Granville Island, leaving plenty of time to linger at one of the many alfresco tables of the city's famous coffee houses, people-watching or simply gazing off into the distance. Take a lunch break at one of the 3,000 or more restaurants that have made the city renowned for fine dining and interesting menus, followed by an afternoon featuring more neighbourhood strolling or downtown shopping. Ultimately, it doesn't matter whether you choose style or substance, for there's no such thing as a wasted day in Vancouver.

Plaques and Statues

As you stroll around Vancouver, keep your eyes open for plaques at historic sites and interesting pieces of statuary and murals. There are hundreds of plaques in the downtown area alone, recalling momentous events in the city's history. You can get a list from City Hall, but it's much more fun to discover them by chance.

There are works of public art throughout the city – *Gassy Jack* in Gastown and *Girl in a Wetsuit* in Stanley Park are famous examples, but there's much more to discover. The Public Art Program has devised two walking routes that encompass some of the best – one circling six blocks of the downtown area, the other following the shoreline of the downtown peninsula (illustrated leaflets available from City Hall).

View from Stanley Park across the bay of Vancouver

STANLEY PARK AND THE WEST END

Even the briefest visit to Vancouver has to include a trip to
Stanley Park. Located next to the vibrant West End, between
English Bay and Burrard Inlet, it's one of the loveliest, most
entertaining and memorable spots around.

Stanley Park

A walk or drive through **Stanley Park** shows why this ver- ◄
dant oasis is regarded as the soul of the city. You can begin
by the seawall, but really any spot will do. If you can borrow
or rent bicycles (rental shops abound on Denman Street),
you can tour all of the park's highlights in less than a day.

Named after the then-Governor General Lord Stanley,
Stanley Park became Vancouver's favourite 405 hectares
(1,000 acres) on 17 September 1888, a mere two years after
the city officially came into existence. Once thickly covered
with cypress, cedar and Douglas fir trees, its forest and

Stanley Park Seawall is a favourite place for keeping fit

shores were the Coast Salish people's hunting and gathering grounds for centuries, before smallpox decimated the indigenous population and European settlers restricted where the remaining First Nations could live.

Preserving the Park

In 1863 the area became a military reserve, and five years later logging companies began cutting the old-growth forest. In 1886, the first city council petitioned the federal government to lease the now-unused military area to the city for a park. Stories about the negotiations tell that the plan was backed by an influential land speculator, aware that preserving such spectacular acreage would only add to the value of his adjacent land. Whether it evolved from self-interest or enlightenment, the park has always shown how balancing quality of life and business interests benefits everyone – a model that has influenced the city's development to this day.

The City's Playground

Devonian Harbour Park is the small, flower-bedecked area above Coal Harbour, which leads to the formal entrance to Stanley Park at the foot of West Georgia Street. You'll see a bronze statue of a woman rummaging through her pocket-book (*The Search*, by J. Seward Johnson, Jr.), one of many examples of public art throughout the city. Any runners you see are headed to the seawall promenade, a 10-km (6-mile) path that rings the park and is an all-seasons attraction for strollers, dog walkers, joggers, skaters and bikers. Along the east side of the promenade are various well-known land-marks including the Vancouver Rowing Club, Royal Vancouver Yacht Club and the '9 o'clock Gun', which once served as a signal for fishermen and continues to remind the citizenry to put the kids to bed. Before venturing on past Brockton Point and the *Girl in a Wetsuit* sculpture, veer off the path to see a collection of Kwakiutl, Tlingit, and Haida totem poles, among the most photographed sites in the city.

From March to October horse-drawn bus tours of Stanley Park are a fun way to see the highlights and pick out places to return to on foot for further exploration. For details, tel: 604/681-5115.

Further on, Lumberman's Arch sits on the site of a former Squamish village, and if you are travelling with youngsters, they'll also enjoy a detour to the **Children's Farmyard** and the **Miniature Railway** (both attractions open Apr–Sept: daily; weekends only Oct–Mar; admission fee).

Around Prospect Point

Expansive views of North Vancouver will propel you around **Prospect Point**, the northern tip of the seawall, where seagulls, grasping their lunch in their beaks, picnic

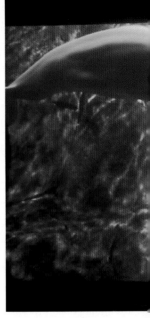

on the rocks. Benches are plentiful if you need a place to rest or just want to soak up the wonderful panorama. As you walk south, you'll see Siwash Rock, with its distinctive lone tree standing sentinel over the water. If you've walked and worked up an appetite for a gourmet meal by this time, you'll be handy for the Sequoia Grill at Ferguson Point *(see page 139)*. Cross Stanley Park Drive at any point on your trek to reach the former logging roads that now serve as trails through the forest. Busy little chipmunks scampering down the thick tree trunks show no fear of humans as they practically knock you over in their quest for an easy snack, leaving you to wonder how they manage through winter with fewer hand-outs.

The Aquarium

Don't bypass the excellent **Vancouver Aquarium Marine Science Centre** (Stanley Park, tel: (604) 659-3474; <www.vanaqua.org>; open daily 10am–5.30pm, admission fee). One of the top aquariums in North America, and Canada's largest. Helpful staff members answer questions and entertain bystanders with odd insects (such as stick insects) in the Amazon Gallery. Massive indoor viewing tanks hold thousands of interesting and exotic species, such as the arapaima, the world's largest freshwater fish. The biggest attraction, in every sense, are the beluga whales in the Arctic

Beluga whale and young spectator at the aquarium

Canada exhibit, and other outdoor attractions include a replicated salmon hatchery and above- and below-water viewing of dolphins, sea lions and seals.

Theatre and Second Beach

Just west of the aquarium are the **Rose Garden** and **Malkin Bowl**, the latter the home of **Theatre Under the Stars** (performances mid-July to mid-Aug). As you head towards the Beach Street entrance to the park, you'll pass **Second Beach** with a playground, snack bar and a heated freshwater pool with a large shallow section and slides. Trails lead to **Lost Lagoon** and the **Nature House** which offers information on park ecology and walking tours.

The West End and Denman Street

Don't confuse the West End with West Vancouver (a suburb across the Lions Gate Bridge) or with the city's West Side (a group of well-to-do districts across the Burrard Street Bridge). In fact, the **West End** is the most densely populated 194 hectares (480 acres) in the whole of Canada. Once filled with gracious homes, the area around Denman Street is now crowded with high-rise apartments and condominiums that house a mixed population, including young singles, professional people, families and a large gay community. In a late-1960s flurry of redevelopment, nine old houses were rescued and relocated to **Barclay Square Heritage Park** at Nicola and Barclay streets. In particular, the 1893 **Roedde House Museum** (1415 Barclay Street, tel: 604/684-7040; call for a schedule; guided tours Tues–Fri at 2pm) is worth a visit. Built in 1893 by the founder of the G.A. Roedde printing company, its design is attributed to the famous civic architect, Francis M. Rattenbury (whose imposing provincial parliament building and the Empress Hotel distinguish the Inner Harbour in Victoria). Restored to its original condition, its displays of period clothing and furniture depict middle-class life in the late 19th century.

Denman Street itself is a vibrant nine-block strip between West Georgia Street and Beach Street, which is home to countless restaurants encompassing pretty much the whole spectrum of world cuisines, as well as nice little neighbourhood cafés. Here you can browse around an eclectic mix of shops that range from trendy to tacky; organise a skydiving adventure or a harbour cruise; get a haircut or visit a tanning salon. It's a vibrant hangout – youthful, funky and jammed with traffic during the rush hour.

The distinctive 'sails' of Canada Place

DOWNTOWN VANCOUVER

No matter which downtown high-rise is casting its shadow on you, you're still only a few minutes' walk from the calming sight of deep blue water – downtown Vancouver has False Creek to the south, Burrard Inlet to the northeast and English Bay to the west. In addition to the main commercial and waterfront districts, the downtown area features such sightseeing gems as historic Gastown, site of the original settlement, and colourful Chinatown.

The Waterfront

Water is the means by which a great many visitors enter Vancouver, but if you didn't arrive by ship, you can replicate the experience with a stroll around the outer decks of **Canada Place**. Built for the 1986 World Expo, its lower levels serve as a convention centre and shopping mall, with the high-rise Pan Pacific Hotel towering above all. Five famous white

If it's raining and you feel in need of a tonic, Vancouver's 19 day spas should keep you relaxed and happy until the clouds subside. Downtown, investigate the holistic, wellness, beauty and anti-aging treatments at La Raffinage (tel: 604/681-9933) or check out the massages and wraps at Spa Sense (tel: 604/685-0411). Among others, Waterfront Centre, Sutton Place, and Fairmont Hotel Vancouver offer spa sevices.

'sails' mark this spot between Howe and Hornby streets. Beyond the deck railings are unobstructed views of the North Shore, but a glance back at the brick buildings lining Gastown might prompt you to imagine Vancouver as it was 100 years ago. For a bird's-eye view of the whole area, take the external lift up the 177-m (581-ft) Harbour Centre Tower to its observation deck, known as **The Lookout**.

Situated nearby, on Cordova Street, is the former Canadian Pacific Railway terminal, **Waterfront Station**. Rebuilt in 1914, this is the place to catch the **SeaBus** to Lonsdale Quay (see page 56), the **SkyTrain** to TELUSphere (see page 44) or the West Coast Express commuter trains out to the suburbs. Take a look inside: the airy station is decorated with murals of the Rocky Mountains, and watching everyone bustling to and fro is energising.

Across the street from Waterfront Station is one of the city's many indoor shopping arcades, the attractive **Sinclair Centre**. An elegant conversion of a heritage building, it contains a good range of shops on two levels, including fashion boutiques, speciality stores and food outlets. It does cater largely for those with a healthy bank balance, but window shopping is fun, too, in the unhurried atmosphere and open design of the building.

Robson Street and the Central Business District

Endlessly touted as the shopping mecca of Vancouver, there's a bit more to Robson Street than the fashionable hordes parading past others dining alfresco on balmy summer nights. While a portion of the street is a melange of retailers, hotels and restaurants, once you cross Burrard Street and head east, things quieten down a little.

Three blocks long, **Robson Square**, a public plaza on Robson Street between Hornby and Howe streets, was designed by renowned architect Arthur C. Erickson in modern geometric design; it is part of a complex that includes the provincial law courts with their distinctive sloping glass roofs. The square's broad, leafy public spaces entice passers-by to linger. At night, a lighted waterfall provides a soothing contrast to the traffic noise, and in the summer months, concerts are held on the plaza.

Leafy Robson Square

Taking a break in central Vancouver

Hornby to Burrard

The old Vancouver courthouse is now the home of the **Vancouver Art Gallery** (750 Hornby Street, tel: 604/662-4719; <www.vanartgallery.bc.ca>; open: Mon–Sat 10am–5.30pm, Thur to 9pm, Sun noon–5pm; admission fee). A fine example of classical architecture, the gallery, the largest in of its kind in western Canada, showcases a wide range of exhibitions, from shows on historical old masters to contemporary pieces. Founded in 1931, it now has around 8,000 works in its collection. Of particular note in the gallery is a floor dedicated to the paintings of Emily Carr, a native of Victoria and one of western Canada's most celebrated artists and writers. Other strong areas in the gallery's collection include photoconceptual work by Stan Douglas, Jeff Wall and Ian Wallace; posters by Lawrence Weiner; prints by American expressionist Leon Golub and the artist Nancy Spero.

Farther down Robson between Homer and Hamilton streets, the relatively new **Library Square** is an awe-inspiring sight. Reminiscent of Rome's Coliseum from the outside, the inside is pure fun, with small shops and coffee outlets partially ringing the entrance to the public library's stacks. Across Homer is the **Centre in Vancouver for the**

Performing Arts, home to travelling musicals and a gift shop selling theatre-orientated trinkets, T-shirts and books.

The verdigris roof of the **Fairmont Hotel Vancouver** on West Georgia and Burrard streets is almost as symbolic of the city as Stanley Park. This is the third incarnation of the hotel, the first having opened in 1887 and been rebuilt in 1916 on Granville and Georgia streets, currently the site of Sears' department store. Construction on the present hotel began in 1928 but wasn't completed until 1939, opening in time to greet King George VI of England. Along with its landmark status, the hotel has a number of exclusive shops.

Continuing a bit down Burrard Street, you come to **Christ Church Cathedral**, an Anglican parish church completed during 1895 and extensively renovated in 2005, including the installation of a new organ. After escaping demolition in the 1970s, the sandstone building became part of lofty **Cathedral Place**, built in 1991. Be sure to notice the glorious art deco stained-glass door on the tower's west side, a relic from the building that this complex replaced.

Moshe Safdie

The architect of the Centre in Vancouver for the Performing Arts has designed some of the most stunning modern buildings in North America and Israel (where he was born). Brought to Canada by his family, he got his architecture degree at McGill University in Montréal, where he later masterminded the 1967 World Exhibition. His work includes Ottawa's National Gallery of Canada and the Museum of Civilisation across the river in Gatineau, Québec; the US Institute of Peace Headquarters in Washington and many projects in Jerusalem, including the restoration of the Old City, reconstruction of the New City, the Yad Vashem Holocaust Museum and Rabin Memorial Centre.

The art deco Marine Building

Art deco aficionados will also appreciate the **Marine Building** at Hastings and Burrard, a masterwork of detail and, with 25 storeys, once the tallest building in the province of British Columbia. Be sure to enter the lobby to admire the stained glass and murals (1929–1930) depicting Vancouver's maritime history.

Gastown

Vancouver's history as a city has its origins in **Gastown**, and yet these 2.5 hectares (6 acres) were left to languish for many decades until community groups and property owners began drawing attention to the area's importance and its great possibilities. In 1971 Gastown was declared a heritage district, and the following year both the federal and provincial governments helped the city to pay for renovations that included the addition of Victorian-style lamp posts, red brick streets and greenery.

Designed with tourists in mind, Gastown's most recent addition is **Storyeum** (142 Water Street, tel: 604/687-8145; <www.storyeum.com>; open Mon–Tues 10am–5pm, Wed–Fri 9.30am–5pm, Sat, Sun and holidays 10.30am–5pm; admission fee), a lively and theatrical, multimedia-learning-through-entertainment attraction that touches on various historical aspects of Vancouver, from West Coast creation myths to the coming of the railway.

The Steam Clock and 'Gassy' Jack Statue

Across the street, visitors seem universally delighted to catch sight of the **Steam Clock** on the corner of Cambie and Water streets. Constructed in 1977 based on an older design, the clock whistles in 15-minute intervals and blows steam on the hour.

Two blocks further down, at Carrall and Water streets, is Maple Tree Square, presided over appropriately by a bronze **statue of John Deighton**, the legendary 'Gassy Jack', who supplied whisky to Vancouver's fledgling populace and was probably the source of the district's name. Rumour has it that with just a single barrel of whisky for collateral, loquacious Deighton built his tavern.

From June to August, free 90-minute guided walking tours of the area are given by the **Gastown Business Improvement Society** (tel: 604/683-5650), leaving from Maple Tree Square at 2pm.

The Steam Clock, Gastown

If you're planning to cross Gastown into Chinatown on foot, head south on Carrall to East Pender to avoid the worst of the city's skid row on East Hastings Street.

Traditional medicinal herbs on sale

Chinatown

The original Chinese immigrants arrived in Vancouver to work in the goldfields and on the railways, and North America's third-largest **Chinatown** has a history dating back to 1858. In the once thriving community of Richmond, a generation of old-timers has died out and made room for the Asian immigrants who have flocked to the suburb, where behemoth concrete shopping malls have replaced the crowded stores lining Pender Street as the place to purchase life's essentials. Commerce in today's Chinatown is nevertheless alive and well, as evidenced by the crowds at the **Night Market** on Keefer and Main streets, open from May through September from 6.30pm to 11.30pm every Friday, Saturday, and Sunday.

The best way to approach Chinatown is to walk the 'Silk Road', which starts at Vancouver Public Library, following the banners to the ornate Millennium Gate. This marks the entrance to Chinatown and leads conveniently to the nearby **Chinese Cultural Centre** (50 East Pender Street), built in 1981, which stands nearby. This community resource hosts Chinese opera and dance events as well as classes and holiday celebrations, and is fronted by a traditional gateway constructed in China for Expo '86.

Chinese Garden

Behind the Chinese Cultural Centre is the delightful **Dr Sun Yat-Sen Classical Garden** (578 Carrall Street, at Keefer Street, tel: 604/662-3207; <www.vancouverchinesegarden. com>; open spring: 10am–6pm; summer: 9.30am–7pm; autumn/winter: 10am–4.30pm; admission fee), a Ming Dynasty-style jewel, complete with traditional buildings that were constructed by artisans from China without a single nail or screw. Volunteer guides add immeasurably to a tour of the garden by describing how Chinese stories and culture influenced the placement of each rock, tree and gate. Try timing your arrival to coincide with a tour – it's an hour well spent.

Allow plenty of time for poking around the fascinating stores (including Chinese herbalists) and colourful markets, admiring the architecture and perhaps indulging in some authentic *dim sum* for lunch. And don't forget to have a look at the huge Han Dynasty Bell in Shanghai Alley and the world's skinniest insurance office, the 2-m (6-ft) wide **Sam Kee Building** on Pender and Carrall streets.

Tortoise, Dr Sun Yat-Sen Garden

FALSE CREEK AND GRANVILLE ISLAND

Until the mid-1850s, the wayward tributary of English Bay called **False Creek** provided generations of the Squamish nation with a living in the form of fishing and hunting. The industrialisation of the shores of False Creek began with lumber mills in the 1860s and continued until the end of World War II, when a combination of troubles (including pollution and factory closures) led to suggestions that the creek be drained. As yet another example of local politics and luck conspiring to benefit the city, False Creek instead became a model of urban renewal.

Granville Island marina

Granville Island

The star of the False Creek redevelopment story is most definitely **Granville Island**. It's not actually an island at all, just a mushroom-shaped piece of land jutting out into the water, accessible by car from the **Granville Bridge** and by ferry from TELUS-phere, Yaletown, and the Hornby Street Pier. A former industrial wasteland, it was saved in 1979 and is a self-contained village with an eclectic and trendy mix of individual stores, craft galleries, restaurants and entertainment venues. The jewel in its crown is the colourful and immensely enjoyable

Granville Island Public Market, with stall after stall heaped with fruit and vegetables, baked goods, meat, fish, gifts, sweets and flowers – a bountiful source for cooks and food-lovers.

Outside the market there's usually a full schedule of street performers, and nearby is the justly popular **Kids Only Market**, a massive collection of toys, books, games, clothing and confectionery. Adults (who, after all, hold the credit cards) are welcome to help the little ones shop; be warned: the video and arcade games on the second floor might interfere with your timetable.

Fresh produce at the Granville Island Public Market

Granville Arts Scene

Former industrial buildings with corrugated roofs also shelter arts and crafts galleries, studios, offices and even an art school named after Emily Carr. The Granville Island Hotel provides cheery lodgings, and a variety of restaurants overlook the bridges, water and seafaring activity.

Granville Island is a popular night spot, too. The **Arts Club Theatre** produces shows throughout the year, and its Backstage Lounge presents a regular roster of live music.

Be forewarned that parking, especially at weekends, is difficult, as is manoeuvring a car through the narrow streets. You can easily take the bus to Granville Island, or leave your car on Pacific Avenue near Hornby Street and take the little **AquaBus** across False Creek.

Yaletown

The southeast edge of False Creek is currently undergoing development into a new residential community but a small nearby area between Nelson and Davie streets has already metamorphosed into a hip and happening district. **Yaletown** (or 'Yaletown High', as some of its residents flippantly call it, referring to its small-town, everyone-knows-everyone feeling) is filled with interesting boutiques, restaurants and clubs. Although it's only two blocks long and two blocks wide, you can easily let an afternoon slip away going from one shop to another with a break for drinks or a meal.

The **B.C. Sports Hall of Fame and Museum** (777 Pacific Boulevard, tel: 604/687-5520; open daily 10am–5pm; admission fee), is located at Gate A of the **B.C. Place Stadium**. The stadium, covered by the world's biggest air-supported dome, hosts concerts and exhibitions as well as the B.C. Lions football team. Dedicated sports fans should pop into the museum for a tour of British Columbia's sports history. Hands-on exhibits allow twitching muscles to get some exercise.

At the end of False Creek is the silver geodesic dome nicknamed the 'golf ball' and now the site of **TELUSphere** (Quebec Street, tel: 604/443 7443; summer: daily 10am– 6pm; winter: Mon–Fri 10am–5pm, Sat and Sun 10am–6pm; admission fee).

Vancouver has a magnificent setting, and dining with a view includes gazing at the North shore mountains, looking out over a marina or enjoying a bird's-eye view from the mountains. When you reserve, ask for a prime viewing spot – not all tables have one.

TELUSphere is a multi-level, almost totally interactive science museum disguised as fun – from fun-house mirrors and computers (always busy), to plasma balls, floating magnets, robotics, mind puzzles and music machines. If you're travelling with children expect to spend two hours there.

Fun in the sun

THE WEST SIDE AND THE EAST SIDE

From downtown, the Burrard Street and Granville Street bridges cross False Creek and lead to Vancouver's **West Side**, a series of neighbourhoods ranging from Shaughnessy Heights, whose early residents were the cream of Vancouver society during the 1920s, to perky Kitsilano, where 1960s bohemians have morphed into the present-day bourgeoisie. A number of worthwhile attractions and pleasant beaches are located on the West Side, not to mention some of the city's most vaunted restaurants.

Kitsilano

Named after Squamish Chief Khahtsahlanough in 1905, **Kitsilano** is a popular district with young, well-to-do families. The main shopping district, Kits, lies on West 4th Street – a terrific collection of home decor, clothing, sporting goods and health-food shops interspersed with a variety of ethnic and high-end restaurants and new residential condominiums and flats.

Vanier Park and Vancouver Museum

Vanier Park, which was a First Nations settlement in the latter half of the 19th century, lies on the shores of English Bay and is accessible off the first Burrard Street Bridge exit. Among the park's charms are the well-designed and interesting Vancouver Museum and the MacMillan Space Centre.

The **Vancouver Museum** (Vanier Park, 1100 Chestnut Street, tel: 604/736-4431; <www.vanmuseum.bc.ca>; open daily 10am–5pm, Thur to 9pm; admission fee) takes you through several thousand years of local history in an accessible and entertaining manner that will appeal to both kids and adults. Start with an Egyptian mummy of a boy collected by a 19th-century Vancouver doctor. Then proceed to the deck

Vanier Park

of a sailing ship, a Hudson's Bay Company frontier trading post, an 1880s railway car, fancy Victorian and Edwardian parlours, and an exhibit of 1940s and 1950s neon signs, from the city's days as the West's glitziest metropolis.

Vancouver Museum's neon signs

The **H.R. MacMillan Space Centre** (Vanier Park, 1100 Chestnut Street, tel: 604/738-7827; <www.hrmacmillanspacecentre.com>; open July–Aug: daily 10am–5pm; Sept–June Tues–Sun; admission fee) shares the premises with the museum. The H.R. MacMillan Planetarium is now modernised and renamed to appeal to 21st-century travellers. There are many intriguing activities at the Space Centre, but if you are shepherding children, be sure to purchase the admission package that includes an exciting ride on the Mars simulator and one of the clever multimedia shows on the solar system situated in the second-floor theatre.

Maritime Museum

Also in Vanier Park is the **Vancouver Maritime Museum** (1905 Ogden Avenue, tel: 604/257-8300; <www.vancouvermaritimemuseum.com>; open: Tues–Sat 10am–5pm, Sun noon–5pm; admission fee), with ship models, photographs and a children's interactive exhibit called the 'Maritime Discovery Centre'. Walk on the Heritage Harbour docks to see the vintage boats and take in the views. During the summer, 'Bard at the Beach' here features a series of Shakespeare plays staged in a marquee overlooking the bay.

Façade of the Maritime Museum, Burrard Street *(see page 47)*

A walking and cycling path will lead you to **Kitsilano Beach Park** between Trafalgar and Maple streets. It has some lovely views and features an outdoor salt-water pool and tennis courts and is where all the healthy young locals spend their days off.

Pioneer Park and Jericho Beach

The 1886 fire that destroyed Gastown spared few buildings, but one that survives now graces **Pioneer Park** in Point Grey at the end of Alma Street. The **Hastings Mill Store** (1575 Alma Road, tel: 604/734-1212; open summer: daily; winter: weekends; free) dates from 1865 and serves as a catch-all museum of relics including an embroidered portrait of Queen Victoria. Nearby, **Jericho Beach Park**, a former military base, is the site of the annual **Vancouver Folk Festival**, held the third weekend in July. There's a youth hostel in former barracks overlooking the water.

Point Grey and the University of B.C.

The exclusive **Point Grey** neighbourhood encompasses two of Vancouver's best beaches, Locarno and Spanish Banks, and the vast campus of the **University of British Columbia** (U.B.C.). Although land for the new university was endowed in 1911 by the government and UBC opened in 1915, classes weren't held at the Point Grey site until 1925.

As you approach the campus on West 4th (which becomes Chancellor Boulevard), you'll notice a great tract of forest. The university had originally intended to develop much of this land for housing, leaving only a small portion of the area's old-growth woodland for a park. A series of unforeseen circumstances conspired to delay the parceling off of lots, including transport difficulties, the Great Depression, shortages during World War II and, in the 1960s and 1970s, community resistance. As a result, the university's plan to destroy the forest never came to fruition. Instead, the 763-hectare (1,885-acre) **Pacific Spirit Regional Park** was officially established in 1988. Its 55km (34 miles) of trails are open to the public for hiking, biking and horse riding – though there really isn't anywhere nearby to procure a horse.

Once inside the university grounds, you'll pass the **Chan Centre for the Performing Arts** (tel: 604/822-2697). These state-of-the-art facilities include a 1,400-seat concert hall with stellar acoustics, a 250-seat studio theatre, and a 160-seat cinema. There's a free tour of the facility offered on Tuesdays and Fridays at 1pm. A schedule of recitals, contemporary and classic plays,

The University of B.C. is justly proud of its beautiful campus and offers guided walking tours (tel: 604/822-8687; late May–end Aug), taking in such attractions as the Belkin Art Gallery, Chan Centre and Anthropology Museum.

and other events can be seen on the Centre's website, <www. chancentre.com>.

It might be stretching a point to say that Arthur Erickson is to modern architecture in Vancouver as Antonio Gaudí is to Modernist architecture in Barcelona. Nevertheless, U.B.C.'s **Museum of Anthropology** (6393 Northwest Marine Drive, tel: 604/822-5087; <www.moa.ubc.ca>; open Wed– Sun 10am–5pm, Tues to 9pm. Also closed 8 Sept– 24 May; admission fee) is one of Erickson's most admired

First Nations

First Nations peoples are surprisingly under-represented when it comes to visitor attractions in Vancouver. Totem poles can be spotted in many tourist sites and parks, but with the exception of the Museum of Anthropology *(see this page)*, there are few places to gather significant details about the culture and history of the Northwest Coast Natives. While the museum's collection is unique and potent, it still leaves the impression of Native culture as belonging to the past.

Happily, the addition on Grouse Mountain of the **Híwus Feasthouse** helps to fill the breach between past and present with an entertaining multimedia programme of native food, stories, song and dance. The evening begins at the Grouse Mountain Lodge, where you meet your guide for an easy hike to the cedar longhouse. Guests are then seated on cushioned chiefs' benches. Between dances and legends performed by local members of the Salish and Musqueam tribes, a multi-course dinner is served in cedar boxes and baskets. The programme ends with the audience participating in a rousing ceremonial dance – one sure way to develop a relationship among cultures. For ticket information, phone Grouse Mountain Guest Services at (604) 980-9311. Currently, the Híwus Feasthouse is open to the public from May to early October.

structures. Built in 1976 on a bluff overlooking English Bay, the museum is a 20th-century rendition of a First Nations longhouse (ceremonial building) with superb natural lighting and a far-ranging collection of West Coast Native art. Guides lead an hour-long tour of the main gallery, providing interesting background on the displays that conclude with the famous carving *The Raven and the First Men*, by Haida artist Bill Reid. Leave time for private exploration after the tour, for the majority of the museum's collections are cleverly displayed in easily accessible glass-

Totem pole in the Museum of Anthropology

topped drawers. Don't miss the **Koerner Ceramics Gallery** at the west end of the building. It contains thousands of contemporary Canadian and European works but is often overlooked by museum visitors.

U.B.C. **Gardens**

Across the street and a short walk away (marked by a small, easy-to-miss sign) is the **Nitobe Memorial Garden** (University of British Columbia campus, tel: 604/822-6038; <www.nitobe.org>; open: daily 10am–6pm, limited hours autumn–winter; admission fee). The small, attractive, and carefully maintained garden features man-made waterfalls and a pond, and there's a teahouse among the trees and shrubs. The university also cultivates the 28-hectare (69-acre) **U.B.C. Botanical Gardens** (6804 Southwest Marine Drive, tel: 604/822-3928; <www.ubcbotanicalgarden.org>; open spring–summer: 10am–6pm; autumn–winter: 10am–5pm; admission fee), divided into five distinct green belts: the British Columbia Native Garden, Asian Garden, Physick Garden, Alpine Garden and Food Garden. The layout can seem confusing, so ask for a map at the entrance. Like most gardens, it's best visited in the spring or summer when the plants are still blooming.

Shaughnessy and Little Mountain

Located on the old Shaughnessy Golf Course about a 15-minute drive from downtown, the **VanDusen Botanical Garden** is a year-round glory. This city-owned, non-profit Eden comprises 22 hectares (59 acres) of theme gardens and a delightfully tricky hedge maze. The multitude of plants along the many paths are all identified, and the park is well-signed and easy to navigate. It's one of the prettiest botanical gardens around. If you happen to be visiting during autumn, you'll be dazzled by the colours of the turning leaves. The gift shop is full of appealing items for horticulturists, and there is a full-service restaurant (Shaughnessy) serving lunch and dinner daily in the shop pavilion.

VanDusen Botanical Gardens

Located slightly further east, on Cambie Street at 33rd, is **Queen Elizabeth Park** (also known as 'Little Mountain'). A former rock quarry, this park marks the high ground as well as the

Bloedel Conservatory

geographical centre of Vancouver. It's a favourite site for wedding photographs; on summer Saturdays you'll no doubt see many a bride traipsing up one of the paths. Along with Seasons in the Park, a restaurant that hosted Boris Yeltsin and Bill Clinton during their 1993 summit, the **Bloedel Conservatory** (Queen Elizabeth Park, 33rd Avenue at Cambie Street, tel: 604/257-8584; <www.city.vancouver.bc.ca/parks>; open: daily 10am–5pm; admission fee) shares the Little Mountain summit and is open year round. Tropical birds fly freely amid the conservatory's rainforest-like setting, which shelters unusual plants collected from all over the world.

At the foot of the mountain on Ontario Street is a 6,500-seat baseball park called **Nat Bailey Stadium**. Fans come here for the summer home games of the Canadians, Vancouver's Short Season-A Pacific Coast League baseball team (see page 89).

The East Side: Commercial Drive

The Grandview neighbourhood on the East Side of Vancouver is referred to as **Little Italy,** but it has traditionally sheltered a diverse working-class population. Just 10 minutes by car from downtown (or take the SkyTrain to the Broadway Station), it is one of Vancouver's more affordable areas (a vanishing breed), with young families increasingly arriving and renovating the pre-World War I homes. The shopping district, centred on **Commercial Drive**, truly reflects both the city's cross-cultural mix and a marvellous vitality. It's one of the areas where you'll see evidence of Vancouver family life and is apparently where the counterculture goes for coffee. A great place to take in the scene is from a table at Havana *(see page 137)*. Then, meander down the street, perhaps collecting a picnic lunch from the local Italian deli or snacks from one of the many bakeries. For dinner, try Dario's in the Italian Cultural Centre.

EXCURSIONS

Day trips beyond the city limits can be as close as a 20-minute drive across the Lions Gate Bridge to North or West Vancouver, or as far as a 12- to 14-hour round-trip to Victoria for those folks determined to sip a cup of tea in the genteel surroundings of the Empress Hotel. The mountains from the North Shore to Whistler offer wintertime skiing and summertime hiking, and vast regional parks are also awash with trails and gorgeous scenery. Hopping on a ferry to one of the islands is another Vancouver activity, one that can be a vacation in itself if you have a few days to spare.

North Vancouver

The shores of **North Vancouver** were the exclusive long-time home of First Nations people until 1862, when a couple of businessmen decided to build a sawmill east of what was

Fabulous views from Whistler

to become the northern end of the Lions Gate Bridge. It was another three decades before the District of North Vancouver managed to incorporate, and at the time there were only a few hundred settlers scattered about the area. Even so, entrepreneurs provided 'ferry' transport (actually a rowing boat) across Burrard Inlet. One pioneering Scotsman, George Grant MacKay, inadvertently built the area's first tourist attraction, the **Capilano Suspension Bridge**. With the completion of the **Lions Gate Bridge** in 1938 and the **Ironworkers' Memorial (Second Narrows) Bridge** in 1960 (the latter is east of Vancouver and part of the Trans-Canada Highway), and the availability of the speedy SeaBus service between the shores, North Vancouver has become a dormitory town for the metropolis across the inlet.

Today, North Vancouver is actually divided into two separate municipalities: North Vancouver District and North Vancouver City; the latter was incorporated in 1907. North

Lions Gate Bridge

'Van' City took the bulk of the spoils when it split off from the District, annexing Grouse Mountain and Lynn Canyon Park. The District, however, encompasses another fine area for hiking, **Mount Seymour Provincial Park**.

The SeaBus leaves from downtown Vancouver's Waterfront Station every 15 to 30 minutes for a short but sweet 12-minute scenic ride across Burrard Inlet to **Lonsdale Quay**. Another boon of Expo '86, Lonsdale Quay is a smaller, less hectic, and more compact version of the Granville Island Public Market. Along with a hotel, there are gift shops, boutiques, restaurants and a full range of fresh goodies to purchase at individual stalls inside the first-floor market.

Lynn Canyon Park

To the west of the ferry dock and behind the market is a bus terminal with connections to **Lynn Canyon Park** (3663 Park Road, North Vancouver, tel: 604/981-3103; <www. dnv.org/ecology>; open daily, summer: 7am–9pm; spring and autumn: 7am–8pm; winter: 7am–7pm; free), among other destinations. Two bus lanes wind through residential neighbourhoods up to the canyon (the No. 229 bus stops almost at the entrance), so there's no real need to drive. The

250-hectare (618-acre) forest offers 161km (100 miles) of hiking trails through dense pines; the only sounds you'll hear (besides other hikers) are birdsong and water splashing over the rocks.

A small **ecology centre** (open: daily 10am–5pm. Closed weekends and holidays Dec–Jan; free) on the main road offers an introduction to forestry, Canadian-style. Lynn Canyon also has its own suspension bridge, a little shorter than the more famous Capilano attraction, but 20 storeys high and just as nerve-wracking – and free. This is the place to test whether you have a fear of heights without first having to make any monetary investment.

Lower Seymour Conservation Reserve

Hikers will be delighted to discover the **Lower Seymour Conservation Reserve** (tel: 604/987-1273; open: daily 8am–5pm, until 9pm in summer; free), which opened to the public in 1987. Located in North Vancouver District at the north end of Lillooet Road (cross the Second Narrows Bridge; exit at Capilano College/Lillooet Road and continue past the cemetery), the site was developed to illustrate forest sustainability and resource management. These are important issues for British Columbia, where approximately 60 percent of the economy depends on this natural resource. At 5,668 hectares (14,005 acres), Lower Seymour Conservation Reserve is 14 times as large as Stanley Park. At weekends, visitors on skates and bicycles share the 11-km (7-mile) gravel road to **Seymour Falls Dam** with pedestrians, but the path is restricted to hikers during the week before 5pm. Vehicular traffic is excluded. **Rice Lake** is stocked with trout (fishing licences are required for adults), and there is an easy walking trail around it that is wheelchair accessible. During the salmon-spawning season, be sure to drive or take the park's shuttle bus to the **Junior Creek hatchery**. It's fascinating to glimpse part of the salmon's life-cycle. On summer Sundays there are free guided walks and bus tours.

Grouse Mountain

A tired-but-true Vancouver cliché informs us that, given the right season, in this locale it's possible to ski in the morning and swim in the sea in the afternoon. **Grouse Mountain**, a 15-minute drive from the city over the Lions Gate Bridge, provides the skiing in this equation, but it's popular after the snow has melted, too. Once you reach the foot of the mountain, there are two ways to get to the top: one is scenic, the other strenuous. The **Grouse Mountain Skyride** (open: daily 9am–10pm, every 15 minutes), an aerial tram that whisks passengers up to 1,100m (3,609ft) over the treetops, provides the views. The hike up to the resort area is a challenging 3-km (2-mile) trek known as the 'Grouse grind', and it's uphill all the way – this is not a walk for the faint-of-heart or out-of-shape. Staff in the information centre can direct you to the trailhead.

At the summit there are yet more hiking trails, a children's playground, a lodge with two restaurants, gift shops and a cinema, plus various attractions. Foremost are the **Refuge for Endangered Wildlife**, currently home to orphaned grizzly bear cubs and some grey wolves, and the **World Famous Lumberjack Show** (May–mid-Oct daily at noon, 2.30pm and 4.30pm), featuring the dazzling skills of two world-class lumberjacks. Besides skiing, winter activities include sleigh rides, ice skating, snow-shoeing and snow-boarding. Summer thrill seekers can paraglide or join a mountain bike tour down the mountain.

Capilano Park and Suspension Bridge

On the way up to Grouse Mountain, you'll pass signs advertising the **Capilano Suspension Bridge** and **Capilano Park** (open: daily from 9am, closing time depends on season;

admission fee). The 137-m (450-ft) cedar bridge, in one variation or another, has been drawing visitors almost since its inception in 1889 and rates as the area's oldest attraction. Touristy though the park is, it's well-designed and hugely appealing, especially to kids. The bridge isn't the sole draw – there are First Nations woodcarvers on site, a large number of totem poles, the Story Centre, with displays about the area, Treetops Adventure, a new elevated treetop boardwalk through the rainforest, a nature park with trails and a trout pond, fast-food counters and one of the largest gift shops you'll ever see. Expect crowds during the high season, as this is one sure stop on every tour-bus schedule.

West Vancouver

If you veer left off the Lions Gate (First Narrows) Bridge onto Marine Drive, you'll discover **West Vancouver**, a resi-

Capilano Suspension Bridge

Point Atkinson Lighthouse

dential community with a reputation for high per capita income. That is not the area's only claim to fame, however. It is also home to Canada's first shopping mall, **Park Royal**, which was constructed in 1950. 'West Van' also sports a seawall promenade like its neighbour across the inlet, but with a twist – here there is a separate pathway for dog-walkers. You can reach the seawall from the delightful **Ambleside Park** (Marine Drive to 13th Street). There are also some terrific restaurants and good shopping along Marine Drive.

Continue west on Marine Drive and watch carefully for the turn into Lighthouse Park. If you're lucky enough to come here out of season or during a work day, you might be treated to a blissfully private walk among old-growth Douglas firs inside this 75-hectare (185-acre) forest. The briefest hike, an easy 10 minutes on the main road, ends at the picturesque **Point Atkinson Lighthouse**, completed in 1912 to replace the 1870s-era original structure.

Travellers can reach the town of **Horseshoe Bay** by taking the bus through West Vancouver. If you aren't planning to take the ferry to Bowen Island, Langdale or Nanaimo, it's quite pleasant to wander around the docks at Horseshoe Bay and watch the boats in Howe Sound. (If you are driving and in a hurry to catch a ferry, be sure to follow the signs to Highway 99; if you take the detour through West Vancouver, it will take double the time.)

Bowen Island

The closest port from Horseshoe Bay is **Snug Cove** on **Bowen Island**, a 20-minute trip by ferry. Nicknamed the 'Happy Isle' by its promoters some 70 years ago, Bowen was the scene of summer picnics and dances in the 1930s that were enjoyed by hundreds of mainlanders who cruised over for an evening's entertainment. Today, many Vancouver sailors dock their craft in the harbour and others have moved to the island to enjoy small-town life and a relatively short commute to the city.

Bowen consists of a tiny but sophisticated shopping area above the docks on the main road with a few restaurants, a bakery, a bookstore, some gift and clothing shops and a gallery. There are a number of activities to pursue here, including hiking in **Crippen Regional Park**, occupying 259 hectares (640 acres) of land that was once controlled by the Union Steamship Company.

A Horseshoe Bay seal

The company's old general store on the site is now a community centre. Two public beaches and a lake are accessible by car, and there are a fair number of bed-and-breakfasts on the island should you be so taken with it that you want to stay for a while.

An especially lovely and invigorating way to enjoy a

few hours here is by kayaking around **Howe Sound**, looking up at the geese or down at the salmon. Bowen Island Sea Kayaking hires the equipment you'll need from an office on the docks and offers the option of a guided tour or lessons *(see page 88)*. Do check weather conditions before setting out, however. Equally wonderful is leaving the car at Horseshoe Bay, walking onto the ferry for a late-afternoon crossing, and having dinner at Blue Eyed Mary's (be sure to make reservations; *see page 142*) before taking the last boat back to Vancouver at 9pm – perfect for a romantic evening.

Howe Sound Activities

Howe Sound is, in fact, a fjord – not the only one on Canada's west coast, but certainly the most southerly, and was formed by glacial action and volcanic activity. It extends inland for 45km (28 miles) from Horseshoe Bay to Squamish, and is followed along its eastern shore by the aptly named Sea to Sky Highway *(see page 64)*.

Locals and visitors alike come here to indulge in all kinds of outdoor activities, including diving among the wrecks offshore, fishing, kayaking (see above) or skimming across the water on a windsurfer or sailing boat. On land there are great hiking trails in the seven provincial parks in the area, challenging climbs on sheer rock faces and some of the best mountain biking in the world – Squamish, at the head of the fjord, is renowned for this activity, with trails of varying difficulty and world-class competitive events.

Every kind of winter sport is available here, even without journeying the extra distance to the Whistler and Blackcomb Mountain resorts, and birdwatchers come each year to see the thousands of bald eagles that converge on the salmon-spawning rivers.

Whistler

Skiers recognise the name **Whistler** immediately and without further explanation. Arguably the premier ski resort in North America, its chalet-style hotels, chalet-style lodges, chalet-style condominium developments, and chalet-style pedestrian-only outdoor shopping centre resemble an illustrated fairytale: 'Once upon a time, there was a village invented solely for the pursuit of leisure activities...'

It's a story that ends happily ever after, if visitor numbers are any indication. More than 2 million arrive from all over the world in the winter to ski down Whistler and Blackcomb mountains, to snowboard, to tramp through the forest on snowshoes, even to fish. In summer the paths around Whistler's five lakes are filled with walkers and cyclists, while year-round ski lifts take hikers up to high elevations for a downhill walk back. Golf enthusiasts can choose from four world-renowned courses around the valley, and tennis players have their pick of resort or public courts. Horse riding is another option; there are small stables in Whistler itself, but for a really magnificent ride head for one of the stables in Pemberton, 35km (28 miles) north of town.

Hiking in Whistler

Even people wanting to relax in less strenuous ways can design a perfect vaca-

Shannon Falls

tion here. **Whistler Village** is filled with shops and restaurants, and most of the resort hotels have full-service health spas, swimming pools, Jacuzzis, video-game rooms and other indoor amenities. There's also a public recreation centre, the **Meadow Park Sports Centre** (tel: 604/935-8350). For a reasonable fee, visitors have access to the indoor swimming pools, sauna, steam room, squash courts, fitness centre, and ice-skating rink.

The Sea to Sky Highway

The journey to Whistler will be a memorable experience in itself. Depending on weather and traffic, the drive from Vancouver takes about two hours on Highway 99, the spectacular 'Sea to Sky' route that hugs the coast as you climb towards the mountains. Take advantage of the many roadside stops in provincial parks which feature small lakes, beautiful creeks, streams and cliffs where rock climbers hone their technique. **Shannon Falls** is a particularly photo-worthy detour, with a dramatic waterfall within sight of the parking area. Once you pass Squamish, don't be misled by the signs indicating your arrival in Whistler. Like many winter resort towns, the road to Whistler is bordered by clumps of condos spread for several miles along the highway. Whistler Village is situated behind one of the last clusters, with parking areas all around one end.

If you aren't driving, you have several other options to reach the mountain. Greyhound Coach Lines (tel: toll-free 800/328-9093) departs eight times a day from the Vancouver bus depot at Main and Terminal streets. Perimeter's Whistler Express (tel: toll-free 877/317-7788) leaves from Vancouver Airport for the three-hour ride to Whistler seven to 11 times daily, depending on the season. You can also charter a helicopter or hire a limousine.

The Village

The area boasts a number of fine restaurants and hotels. Certainly the most lavishly praised is the luxurious **Fairmont Chateau Whistler Resort** at the base of Blackcomb Mountain. It's quite a sight, nearly as imposing as the mountain itself, and if you don't happen to be staying there, be sure to stop in to look around or have a drink. The Village is bursting with high-line ski and sportswear stores, and such standbys as Gap, Levi's and the ubiquitous Starbucks.

The town operates a very well-oiled tourism call centre

Outdoor attractions

Skiing on Blackcomb Mountain

(tel: 800/944-7853 toll-free in Canada and the US, 604/664-5625 elsewhere; <www.tourismwhistler.com>), where friendly operators will assist you with lodging reservations. Information on outdoor activities as well as detailed recreation maps of Whistler are available from the **Whistler Visitor Info Centre** (4230 Gateway Drive, tel: 604/932-5528 ext. 17; <www.whistlerchamber.com>) and the **Whistler Activity Centre** (4010 Whistler Way, tel: 604/938-2769 or 1-877/ 991-9988; <www.tourismwhistler.com>).

Steveston

This quaint fishing village on the edge of the Fraser River's south arm is awash with history. About a 30-minute drive from downtown Vancouver, **Steveston** is the largest commercial fishing port in Canada. But from the late 1890s until World War II, it was also the thriving centre of the canning industry. To gain some understanding of the importance of the fishing industry in British Columbia and how it affected the lives of the local population – once primarily Japanese – start your tour at the **Gulf of Georgia Cannery** (12138 4th Avenue, tel: 604/664-9009; <www.gulfofgeorgiacannery. com>; open June–3 Sep: daily 10am–5pm; 4 Sep–May: Thur–Mon 10am–5pm; admission fee). The biggest operation in Steveston's heyday, it's now a protected heritage site, with exhibits on the history of West Coast fishing, including a short film, a children's activity area and a fascinating scale model of the canning process from fish to finish.

The tiny **Steveston Museum** (open daily for self-guided tours) and Post Office on Moncton Street, in a 1906 prefabricated structure that once housed a bank, presents a bit of turn-of-the-20th-century life and some photographs of the once rowdy town.

Farther east, at the end of Railway Avenue, is the **Britannia Heritage Shipyard,** a working shipyard where you can watch wooden boats being repaired and built.

On the Coast

Another attraction in Steveston is **Vancouver Whale Watch** (tel: 604/274-9565; May–Oct), with speedy Zodiac craft taking you out among the Gulf Islands in the Strait of Georgia to spot the orcas, porpoises, sea lions and bald eagles. A professional naturalist leads the way, armed with a hydro-phone so you can listen to the animals underwater. The company also operates a more leisurely 35-minute guided tour of Steveston Harbour on the *River Queen*.

The waters off British Columbia's coast are home to a resident population of orcas (killer whales). Sightings of these splendid creatures are most common from May to November, when the salmon (their favourite food) are spawning.

Be sure to sample the fish and chips, sold by competing eateries around **Steveston Landing** on Bayview Street, as well as on the *River Queen*. A full day in the Steveston area must also include a hike or ride on the paths through **Garry Point Park** along the shore. Hire bikes at Steveston Bicycle on Chatham Street (tel: 604/271-5544).

Vancouver Island

Vancouver Island, the largest island off North America's west coast, is just 64km (40 miles) from the mainland, separated from Vancouver by the Strait of Georgia to the east and from Washington State in the USA by the Strait of Juan de Fuca to the south and southeast. The island is 515km (320 miles) long, with a population of approximately 689,000, nearly half of whom live in the Greater Victoria area.

Like the mainland, Vancouver Island was home to First Nations peoples for thousands of years and came under British rule, via the Hudson's Bay Company, with the building of Fort Victoria on the southern tip of the island in 1843. Five years later, Britain leased the island to Hudson's Bay with the stipulation that the company establish English colonies there. A few hundred pioneering souls did settle on farms around Victoria, but it was the 1858 Gold Rush that propelled the town from a backwater into the bustling capital of the new province of British Columbia.

> **On Vancouver Island, the salmon swim upstream to their breeding grounds. The chinook, which can weigh up to 36kg (79lb), is the king of all the Pacific salmon.**

Victoria

There are various ways of getting to Victoria from Vancouver. Options include the ferry, plane, seaplane and helicopter.

The fastest (and most expensive) way to go is by air. Harbour Air seaplanes (tel: 604/274-1277 in Vancouver; toll-free 800/665-0212; <www.harbour-air. com>) and Helijet International (tel: 604/273-4688 in Vancouver; toll-free 800/665-4354; <www.helijet.com>) both offer 30-minute one-way harbour-to-harbour flights daily. Air Canada (tel: toll-free 888/247-2262; <www.aircanada.ca>) also has regular scheduled flights between Vancouver International and Victoria International airports.

B.C. Ferries (tel: toll-free 888/223-3779; reservations 604/444-2890 or toll-free 888/724-5223; <www.bcferries. com>) offers frequent 1½-hour cruises between the ferry terminal at Tsawwassen and Swartz Bay.

Daytrippers must keep in mind that driving from downtown Vancouver to Tsawwassen and from Swartz Bay to Victoria will add another 1½ hours one-way, making a driving trip to Vancouver Island a rather long day. Of course visitors do it all the time: by bus, on escorted tours or in their own cars. If you just want to hit the surface of Victoria with a stop at the Butchart Gardens, check with Pacific Coach Lines (tel: toll-free 800/661-1725) or one of the many other charter bus companies making this run.

Vancouver Island's Long Beach

British Columbia's capital is a 30-minute drive from the ferry terminal at Swartz Bay through bucolic countryside – until you reach Victoria's suburbs, that is: a thick, confusing development of housing, shopping malls and fast-food restaurants. But persevere through the suburbs on Highway 17 and you will get to one of the loveliest city centres anywhere, with its downtown business district right by the picturesque inner harbour.

Victoria, once a modest and quaint village beloved for its British pretensions, now suffers somewhat from its own overwhelming popularity. Old town streets are still flower-bedecked, but they are also stuffed with innumerable shops catering for summer-time crowds which will either delight or horrify, depending on your perspective. Even the imperious **Empress Hotel** has seen fit to change with the times. Built by the Canadian Pacific Railway in 1908, this venerable hotel was remodelled in 1987, adding a conference centre. Modernisation aside, taking tea here has always been viewed as a valid reason to make a trip to Victoria, but be prepared for a queue and exorbitant prices.

Victoria's Parliament Building

The Inner Harbour

A walk along the inner harbour and over the Johnson Street Bridge is a splendid way to begin a tour of the city. Many of Victoria's famous heritage buildings can be viewed here, including the Empress and the distinguished 1898 **Parliament Buildings**, all designed by Francis Rattenbury. The **Visitors' Information Centre** (812 Wharf Street, tel: 250/953-2033) is also just north of the bridge on the waterfront. A delightful alternative to a bus tour at this point would be to take the 45-minute harbour tour on the **Victoria Harbour Ferry**. Passengers are entitled to disembark (and climb back on board) at any of the 10 stops along the way, including Chinatown and the **Point Ellice House** (2616 Pleasant Street, tel: 250/380-6506),

The Scandalous Mr Rattenbury

Francis Mawson Rattenbury, who designed many of Victoria's most famous structures, including the Parliament Buildings, the Empress Hotel and the Crystal Palace, was as much a victim of Victorian mores as he was a proponent – at least architecturally. Rattenbury arrived in Victoria from England in 1892 at the age of 25. The young and brash architect's reputation was soon made when he won the competition to design the city's Parliament Buildings. 'Ratz', as he was nicknamed, went on to conceive private and public buildings across the province.

Whether success went to his head, or he succumbed to a midlife crisis, the second half of his life didn't go as smoothly as the first. In his mid-50s, the much celebrated Rattenbury left his wife for a younger woman, the multi-married, cigarette-smoking and lovely Alma Packenham. Naturally, Victoria society snubbed the couple, and so they moved back to England, where Alma took up with their 17-year-old chauffeur, George Stoner. In 1935, fearing that Rattenbury knew of their affair, Stoner clubbed the 68-year-old architect to death as he slept in an armchair. Alma committed suicide days after she was acquitted of murder, and Stoner, who had been sentenced to hang, was eventually released from prison.

where you'll have another opportunity to enjoy an afternoon tea (summers only, Thur–Sun) in the gardens of this lovely Victorian heritage house.

Two-hour guided walking tours of the Inner Harbour or Old Town are available through the **Architectural Institute of British Columbia**. The free tours are given early in the afternoon (except Sun and Mon) in July and August from the Blue Carrot Café in Bastion Square, but you must reserve a space by calling the Vancouver office (tel: 604/683-8588, or toll-free in B.C. only 800/667-0753, ext. 333).

Downtown and the Royal B.C. Museum

To explore independently, set off down **Government Street**, which links up with every point of interest in the small downtown Heritage District. Some of the shops worth a second look include Munro's, a much admired bookshop, and Rogers' Chocolates – a treat for adults and a great incentive for recalcitrant young sightseers.

The **Royal British Columbia Museum** (corner of Belleville and Government streets, tel: 250/387-3014; open: daily 9am-5pm) is one of the finest museums in North America, and features high-impact experiential exhibits on the prehistory, history and natural history of B.C. and the regional First Nations people. A National Geographic IMAX Theatre connected to the museum offers spectacular large-format films about nature, up-close and personal.

Two blocks west on Belleville Street, the **Royal London Wax Museum** has a collection of wax models of various famous and infamous celebrities, along with some lesser-known

Thunderbird Park, behind the Royal B.C. Museum, contains a superb collection of totem poles, displaying the carving skills of people of the Northwest Coast nations.

Enjoying the Canadian summer

politicians. Another Rattenbury-designed building, the **Crystal Garden**, is on the corner of Belleville and Douglas streets; come here to see tropical birds and plants.

Bastion Square and Chinatown

Continue down Government Street to Fort Street for a look around **Bastion Square**, the site of the original Fort Victoria. Here, at No. 28, you will find the excellent **Maritime Museum of British Columbia** (tel: 250/385-4222; open: daily 9.30am–4.30 or 5pm; admission fee), which covers years of seafaring history. More restored 19th-century buildings are scattered along Yates Street, including the 1877 Deluge Fire Company Hall at 636 Yates. Victoria's **Chinatown**, the oldest such enclave in Canada, is just another few blocks away on Fisgard Street. Tiny Fan Tan Alley, once the site of opium dens and gambling parlours, no longer has the sheen of naughtiness about it, but you can use your imagination.

Brilliant bloom at Butchart Gardens

Horse-drawn carriages line Menzies Street beside the Legislative Buildings, waiting to clip-clop customers through a neighbourhood of restored Victorian homes, including that of eccentric artist/author Emily Carr (1871–1945) at 207 Government Street. Continuing on foot, walk south along Douglas Street to **Beacon Hill Park**. Flanked by Dallas Street and with expansive views of the ocean, this 74-hectare (183-acre) green oasis dates from 1852, when it was declared a recreational reserve by James Douglas.

Glorious Gardens

The **Butchart Gardens** (800 Benvenuto Avenue, Brentwood Bay, tel: 250/652-5256 or toll-free 866/652-4422; open: daily from 9am; admission fee), 21km (13 miles) north of Victoria off Highway 17 on the Saanich Inlet, are another reason why people have been flocking to Victoria for generations. Robert Butchart arrived at Tod Inlet in 1902 and set up a branch of the family's cement business. In 1904 his wife Jennie, a keen gardener, began the transformation of his worked-out quarry, planting flowers and shrubs and installing statuary and a fountain. As the gardens expanded, so did their reputation. By 1930 Jennie Butchart had hosted thousands of visitors, and today nearly a million people flock here each year. Still family-owned, the site includes the original sunken garden in the quarry, a rose garden, and Italian and Japanese gardens, the latter having some stunning red maples and old copper beech trees. The concert lawn hosts summer musical events and Saturday evening fireworks. Summer brings many tour buses, though, and the wait for a table in the restaurants here can be lengthy.

On the way to Butchart Gardens, you'll pass a low-slung concrete building on the corner housing the **Butterfly Gardens** (1461 Benvenuto Avenue, tel: 250/652-3822 or toll-free 877/722-0272), a plant-filled humid greenhouse that's home to *Lepidoptera* of all sizes and shapes.

Sooke

If you have a car and time to explore, Highway 14, the West Coast Road, will take you to the little fishing village of **Sooke**, 45km (28 miles) from Victoria. It's close enough to visit for a day, but worth an overnight stay. The **Sooke Harbour House** *(see pages 134 and 142)* is one of many inns in the area, and is among the top dining spots in all of Canada.

Signs indicating Sooke 'potholes' do not refer to a poor road surface, but to natural rock pools in the Sooke River, which is popular for bathing and picnicking. Hikers will enjoy **East Sooke Regional Park**, where trails lead to beaches and an abandoned copper mine; for a challenging day hike, try the 10-km (6-mile) East Sooke Coast Trail. The staff at the **Sooke Museum/Information Centre** on Phillips Road (off Highway 14) can give directions to this and other parks and beaches.

WHAT TO DO

Whether you lean towards physical activity, artistic pursuits, shopping or late-night club hopping, Vancouver is well equipped to meet your needs. While the city might not be considered a mecca of cultural sophistication when compared with, say, New York or London, there's always something happening and somewhere stimulating to go. Given its status as one of the most habitable and attractive cities in the world, Vancouver is a regular stop for touring musicians and theatrical shows. But what makes it a lively place day and night is the sheer number of residents eager to make the most of their after-work hours.

ENTERTAINMENT AND NIGHTLIFE

The weekly *Georgia Straight* newspaper is the best source for entertainment listings if you want to investigate the thriving club and lounge scene around the city. For the ever-growing number of venues that require pre-planning (for example: theatres, concert halls and top jazz clubs), find out what's scheduled during your stay by calling Vancouver's 24-hour Arts Hotline (tel: 604/684-2787) or check their web site at <www.allianceforarts.com>.

Classical Music and Opera

You'll find many outlets for classical music in the city. The Vancouver Symphony Orchestra performs at the glorious **Orpheum Theatre** (Granville Street at Smithe Street, tel: 604/876-3434), which opened in 1927, and in various outdoor locations during the summer. The Vancouver Recital Society brings a mix of talented musicians to the **Vancouver**

The great outdoors is right on the city's doorstep

Playhouse (Hamilton Street at Dunsmuir Street, tel: 604/602-0363), and you'll want to find out who's performing at the acoustically and architecturally brilliant **Centre in Vancouver for the Performing Arts** (777 Homer Street, tel: 604/602-0616). The Vancouver Opera Association produces five full-length operas each season at the **Queen Elizabeth Theatre** (tel: 604/683-0222).

Theatre and Pop Concerts

Live theatre runs the gamut from professional Broadway road companies to local groups performing chestnuts of world drama. Big touring companies tend to come to the **Queen Elizabeth Theatre** (Hamilton and Dunsmuir streets), while you'll find a wide range of concerts – dance, comedy, jazz, blues, pop and more exotic groups – at the adjoining **Vancouver Playhouse** as well as at the **Orpheum** (Smithe and Seymour). For all three, call 604/665-3050. The **Arts Club Theatre** on Granville Island, slightly more casual, is the place to see revivals of classic plays. After years of planning and a $9 million renovation, the Arts Club opened its newest space, the 650-seat **Stanley Theatre** (2750 Granville Street, tel: 604/687-1644). Catch musicals, revues and dramas featuring Canadian writers and artists in this former cinema.

Summer visitors also have two outdoor stages to enjoy. For Shakespeare lovers, borrow a cushion and hie thee to Vanier Park for **Bard-on-the-Beach** (tel: 604/739-0559), where three plays are performed in repertory throughout the summer inside marquees with the loveliest backdrop imaginable – English Bay. Over in Stanley Park, local actors mingle with semi-professionals under the banner of **Theatre Under The Stars** (Malkin Bowl, tel: 604/687-0174), where performances of old Broadway favourites are given in July and August. Those in the know recommend umbrellas, mos-

Hanging out on Granville Street

quito repellent, and a cushion to sit on. If you crave the less conventional, such as new theatre, performance art, jazz, exotic dance or comedy, the **Vancouver East Cultural Centre** (1895 Venables Street, tel: 604/254-9578), known as the 'Cultch', is the place. Housed in a former church, it's an intimate hall with an eclectic crowd, and programmes include children's theatre and chamber music. Also check out the **Firehall Arts Centre** (280 East Cordova Stree, tel: 604/689-0926) for provocative, innovative performances.

Dance

Contemporary and classical dance fans who visit outside the summer months have the opportunity to see a variety of dance companies at the **Queen Elizabeth Theatre** or at the **Firehall Arts Centre**. In July, look for the two-week **Dancing on the Edge Festival**, with cutting-edge choreography performed on street corners and on more traditional stages.

Call Tickets Tonight (tel: 604/684-2787) for schedules and ticket information.

Film

Movies are big business here, both on screen and around town, since Vancouver has become the third most popular city for film-making after Los Angeles and New York City. Granville Street between Georgia and Smithe streets supports a number of multi-screen, first-run movie complexes. For international and 'art' films, the **Pacific Cinematheque** (1131 Howe Street, tel: 604/688-3456) is the local cinemaphile's choice. If you've never experienced one of those larger-than-life, big-sound, wraparound, special-format screens that end in '-max', there are two in Vancouver: the **Omnimax Theatre** at TELUSphere *(see page 44)* and an **IMAX Theatre** at Canada Place *(see page 33)*. A visit to either makes a good outing on a wet day.

Clubs

As evidenced by the throngs of young people lining up to get into some of the more popular night spots, Vancouverites (and energetic 19-year-olds from the States who can legally drink alcohol here) just love a party. You may want to assess the patrons waiting patiently in the rope line before paying any cover charges, especially if kids in disco wear make you giggle. Again, the *Georgia Straight* gives a fairly accurate description of the clubs, but different nights generally attract different crowds.

Blues fans will undoubtedly appreciate **The Yale** (1300 Granville Street, tel: 604/681-9253), a funky, brick-walled bar with a dance floor and a reliable line-up of local and travelling musicians. The **Fairview Pub** (898 West Broadway, tel: 604/872-1262) is another casual club that features good lively blues bands and dancing, and a no-smoking policy, except for an isolated cubicle. The Arts Club Theatre's **Backstage Lounge** on Granville Island also regularly schedules blues musicians, and provides an atmosphere that is comparatively upmarket.

You'll find more adults at these lounges than at some of the other well-advertised clubs such as **Richard's on**

Vancouver Goes to the Movies

If you notice a group of large white trailers hogging all the parking spaces on city streets, it means a movie or television show is being filmed nearby. The motion picture industry began a flirtation with British Columbia in the 1920s, shooting *The Alaskan* in 1924 and footage for *Rosemarie* in 1936, among others. But despite the area's varied and gorgeous scenery, stardom eluded the province until the late 1970s.

Producers began taking the region seriously when they discovered the low Canadian dollar had a positive effect on production costs. British Columbia, sensing the beginnings of a beautiful relationship, hustled to provide facilities and crews. Film-making now accounts for over half a billion dollars for the local economy and employment for approximately 25,000 British Columbians.

A few of the movies filmed in B.C. include *Five Easy Pieces*, *McCabe and Mrs Miller*, *Carnal Knowledge*, *Little Women*, *The Scarlet Letter*, *Jumanji*, *Legends of the Fall*, *This Boy's Life* and *The Accused*. TV's *The X-Files* was shot in Vancouver until recently, and television shows currently produced in and around the city include *Outer Limits*, *So Weird*, *The New Addams Family*, and *Millennium*.

Hoping to see those trailers? The B.C. Film Commission regularly publishes a list of movie projects currently in production, which are available for the taking at the B.C. Business Information Centre, The Station, 601 West Cordova, or by visiting their website: <www.bcfilmcommission.com>.

Richards (1036 Richards Street, tel: 604/687-6794), where a huge space features revolving mirror balls, bulky bouncers and pulsating music – a bit over the top unless you're 20, in which case you might think it's cool. And speaking of cool, **Bar-None** in Yaletown (1222 Hamilton Street, tel: 604/689-7000) and **BaBalu** at the Comfort Inn Downtown (formerly the Hotel Dakota) *(see page 128)* are two of the current trendy spots for drinking. Pool players can try for a table at the **Yaletown Brewing Company** *(see page 137)*. For a sedate evening, try the **Gerard Lounge** at the Sutton Place Hotel *(see page 131)* or the **Wedgewood Hotel Lounge** *(see page 131)*. Both have pianists playing, and you won't feel out of place in a suit or a cocktail dress.

SHOPPING

The shopping's great in Vancouver, but don't expect to stock up on bargains unless you have a favourable exchange rate or you happen to be in town after Boxing Day when the winter sales begin. For souvenirs, don't overlook museum gift shops, which often have a much more varied selection of knick knacks and some excellent handicrafts than the tourist-orientated stores.

What to Buy

Books

Per capita, British Columbians read more than any other group of Canadians, and you'll find well-stocked bookshops downtown and in every neighbourhood. British Columbia's largest is the **University of B.C. Bookstore** at 6200 University Boulevard. Cookbook aficionados should definitely look into **Barbara-Jo's Books to Cooks** at 1128 Mainland Street in Yaletown. The new-age bookstore, **Banyen Books**, at 3608 W 4th Avenue in Kitsilano is a good place for meeting like-minded people.

Clothing

There is a plethora of quality men's clothiers in the **Pacific Centre Mall** (West Georgia Street at Hornby), due to its proximity to the financial centre of the city. There's also an entrance in this mall to **Holt Renfrew**, a modest department store stocking an expensive but prime range of apparel and shoes for men and women. After surveying the shopping areas here, on Robson Street or in any major mall, you might decide most shops resemble each other. However, one small chain is worth mentioning as it sells clothes designed and manu-

Minimalist fashions

factured locally. Called **A-Wear**, their store in the **Sinclair Centre** *(see page 34)* is handsome and staffed with helpful salespeople. And over on the East Side, tucked into Commercial Drive's mix of produce stands, delicatessens and funky shops, lies one terrific Italian shoe shop.

Gifts, Food and Furnishings

Robson Street has long been considered the place for visitors to shop, and while it holds a wide variety of shops and many recognisable labels, there is also a strong element of 'tourist trapism' along the way. Still, you'll want to walk its length from Burrard to Denman just for the experience and to gape at the crowds. Do stop at the **Lush** outlet, which is one in an international chain of soap shops and a very enticing place to stock up on delicious-smelling natural balms and bath items. There are a number of places selling smoked salmon, but sample the goods first before shipping any off as gifts from the Pacific Northwest. For a taste of old Vancouver (by way of Scotland), try **Murchies** at 825 West Pender for coffee and tea and the wherewithal to brew them (one of six Murchies outlets).

Yalestown and Granville

In the 1980s the warehouses of **Yaletown** became trendy restaurants, boutiques, cafés and artists' residences. The shopping there leans towards home decor and clothing shops. Another enjoyable street for browsing is West 4th in **Kitsilano** between Burrard and Alma streets, essentially a neighbourhood shopping district, with everything from a local natural foods grocery to sporting goods.

Granville Island, popular with locals and visitors alike, is busy – especially at weekends, when it's best to arrive via public transport to avoid parking hassles. The **Public Market** here carries all manner of fresh produce: flowers, fish, meat and really anything else one could desire in the way of food. There's also an excellent coffee bar, plus stalls selling bread, chocolate and pastries. It's the place to browse for breakfast or to create a picnic lunch. In adjacent converted warehouses, you'll find crafts, blown glass, textiles and other handmade works of art displayed and sold in small galleries; many of the artists here maintain studios on the island. If you have children in tow, be prepared to settle in for a few hours in the **Kids Only** department store across from the Granville Island Brewery. The second floor features an arcade in which players collect tickets for points scored in the games, to be redeemed for trinkets at a nearby counter, a lengthy exercise for indecisive little ones.

Colourful stand in Gastown

South Granville from 16th Avenue to the bridge is one of the trendiest places to shop. It's a good place to browse for antiques, and is also known for its designer fashions and accessories, high-end gifts and home wares. Just walk up and down until it's time for a coffee. You won't have far to go to find a peaceful pavement café.

Gastown

Gastown is the prime consumer location for T-shirts, Maple Leaf key chains and other 'Guess Who Visited Vancouver?' items. There are also some good jewellery and clothing shops, plus two superb government-licensed galleries specialising in Northwest Coast and Inuit arts and crafts – the **Inuit Gallery of Vancouver** (206 Cambie Street) and **Images for a Canadian Heritage** (164 Water Street), both of which have masks and totems, soapstone and wood carvings, paintings and bentwood boxes.

SPORTS

It's quite exhausting just thinking about the variety of sporting activities available around a city that never stays indoors for too long. In brief, if the sport's been invented, you can probably find somewhere to try it in Vancouver.

On Land
Cycling

You can easily hire bicycles and helmets (required by law) on Denman or Georgia streets near Stanley Park and spend a day biking around the city or park. The River Road bike path in Steveston, reached on the west side of the Dunsmuir Bridge, is lengthy and flat and makes an easy ride for kids.

Hiking and Walking

Within the city limits, Stanley Park has easy forest trails and the 10-km (6-mile) seawall path should be part of every itinerary. You can also walk in Pacific Spirit Park *(see page 49)* beside the UBC campus. For a leisurely stroll, there's the 5-km (3-mile) path through Vanier Park to Jericho Beach.

Hiking country

Outside the city, you have mountains and forests to choose from. Lighthouse Park in West Vancouver ends at an old lighthouse with stunning views of the city after a 10-minute walk through virgin temperate rainforest. And you needn't return to the car once you reach Point Atkinson: there are additional trails to explore here with equally exceptional

Cycling: a great way to explore

vistas. There's a strenuous hike up Grouse Mountain (often closed due to storm damage, *see page 58*), or you can take the chairlift to the Black Mountain trails in Cypress Provincial Park further west. For other day hikes, try Lynn Canyon Park *(see page 56)* or Lower Seymour Conservation Reserve *(see page 57)*.

Golf

Within the city limits, the **University Golf Club** (5185 University Boulevard, tel: 604/224-1818) is open to all, or try the **Furry Creek Golf and Country Club** near Horseshoe Bay or the lovely courses in Whistler and Pemberton.

Skiing

The inveterate skier already knows about Whistler and Blackcomb Mountain in what the travel magazines describe as the finest ski area in North America *(see page 63)*. Even

Britain's Prince William is a fan of these slopes. But for the day skier or for anyone who just wants to play around a bit in the snow, Grouse Mountain, Mount Seymour and Cypress Bowl on the North Shore provide a quick fix. Each place also operates a ski, snowboard and snowshoe school.

On the Water
Kayaking
It's not difficult to learn the basics of sea kayaking quickly. Novices to the sport can take a lesson at the **Ecomarine Ocean Kayak Centre** on Granville Island (tel: 604/689-7575) or on Bowen Island at **Bowen Island Sea Kayaking** (tel: 604/947-9266 or toll-free 800/605-2925) who also offer bike rentals and tours. Then you can set off to paddle around in the bay or Howe Sound, either escorted or on your own and enjoy the great views from the water.

Sea kayaking right in the city

Swimming

The beaches from English Bay to Spanish Banks offer fine saltwater swimming; lifeguards are on duty during the summer months. Kitsilano Beach pool is open from May to September and the pool at Second Beach is open in the summer. The facilities at the Vancouver Aquatic Centre in the West End, including an Olympic-sized indoor pool, are open all year.

Fishing and Sailing

Whale-watching charter boat companies are located in Steveston. One is **Vancouver Whale Watch** (tel: 604/274-9565; <www.vancouverwhalewatch.com>). For yacht cruises and sport fishing, check the charter boats at Coal Harbour beside the Westin Bayshore.

Spectator Sports

Baseball

Vancouver is home to the Short Season-A Vancouver Canadians. During the season (April to October), games are played in the 7,000-seat Nat Bailey Stadium. Tickets may be purchased at the stadium on game days, but call first to check availability (tel: 604/872-5232).

Canadian Football

B.C. Place (tel: 604/589-7627) is the venue for B.C. Lions games from June to October. Tickets may be purchased through Ticketmaster (tel: 604/280-4400).

Hockey

The Vancouver Canucks usually make the play-offs in the National Hockey League, and are the most popular sports team in the city. If you get tickets to a home game at GM Place Stadium, it's sure to be exciting. The season lasts from September to April (tel: 604/899-4625).

CHILDREN

On the windows of various Vancouver attractions, you might notice stickers indicating that the premises are especially suitable for children, as designated by the 'Kid Friendly Vancouver' group. In fact, the entire city pretty much qualifies. Vancouver is a children's paradise, with plenty of outdoor activities and relatively few 'educational' opportunities to ruin an otherwise good time. In addition, the transport possibilities via AquaBus, SeaBus, SkyTrain and ferry all add to the excitement of discovering a new city.

Vancouver's Children's Festival

One annual event underscores Vancouver's fondness for its youngest residents: the Vancouver International Children's Festival, now over 20 years old. For a solid week in May, two dozen red-and-white striped tents take over Vanier Park. They cover the stages that present theatre, music, dance, storytelling and puppet shows by children's performers from across Canada and around the world.

Enhancing the performances are local talent (children's choruses and dance groups), food booths and a marketplace selling books, T-shirts and musical instruments. Festival sponsors underwrite special workshop tents where attendees can make kites, create art and costumes from recycled materials, play music or get their hands on 40,000 Legos.

Vancouver's festival is the prototype on which similar celebrations for children have been modelled all over the world. Like the city that inspired it, it continues to evolve, most recently introducing the 'X-Site', with theatre, visual arts and literary arts programming for teenagers. For information or the festival brochure, contact the organisers (tel: 604/708-5655) or check out their website at <www.vancouverchildrensfestival.com>. Tickets can be purchased through Ticketmaster (tel: 604/280-4444; <www.ticketmaster.ca>).

Beaches and Pools

If the weather's good, any of the beaches from **English Bay** to **Spanish Banks** to **Kitsilano** beg to be explored. In particular, **Second Beach** in Stanley Park has a playground for small children and a wonderful pool with water slides. The **Newton Wave Pool** (13730–72 Avenue, Surrey, tel: 604/501-5540) is another fun water-based option.

Fun in the Whistler snow

Animal Attractions

The **Vancouver Aquarium** *(see page 30)*, with colourful fish, strange insects and regular Beluga whale shows, is a must, especially if you can join in one of the occasional 'sleepover' events. On a smaller, but still fishy scale, there's the **Capilano Fish Hatchery** in Capilano Park *(see page 58)*, where you can witness the lifecycle of the salmon. Kids get a 'passport' at the entrance, which can be stamped at different points in the park and redeemed for a certificate in the gift shop – an effective way to keep the kids moving. **Greater Vancouver Zoo**, on the road to Abbotsford, is a 48-hectare (120-acre) park with masses of animals from around the world where you can spend a full and satisfying day.

Amazing Mazes

The **VanDusen Botanical Garden** is sure to provide some fun with its Elizabethan hedge maze, or you can get lost for much longer in the **Cloverdale Maze** (tel: 604/576-8997; summer only) in the suburb of Surrey.

Celebrating Chinese New Year

Museums

If you think kids will be bored by museums, let them loose with the hands-on exhibits at **TELUSphere** (where there are also live science shows aimed at young visitors) and the **Maritime Museum**, and take them to the humorous planetarium show at the **Pacific Space Centre**. Kids also enjoy the **B.C. Museum of Mining** at Britannia Beach, especially wearing a hard hat for the exciting underground train ride.

Mountain Fun

The gondola ride up **Grouse Mountain** is fun for all the family, and when you reach the top kids will be enthralled by the animals at the wildlife refuge and the film about baby grizzlies at the Theatre in the Sky. Round off the day with a First Nations' style dinner with traditional dancing at Hiwus Feasthouse (tel: 604/980-9311). If you go to **Whistler**, the kids can let off lots of steam in the Adventure Zone, with its rides, trampolines, trapezes and other fun attractions.

Attractions for Tots and Teens

Younger children might well insist you make the 90-minute drive from Vancouver to **Dinotown**, near Bridal Falls, with its dinosaur-themed rides, live shows, paddle boats, pedal cars and street parades.

Teenagers will be happier at Burnaby's **Playdium**, where more than 200 of the latest high-tech console and table games and virtual experiences are on offer.

Festivals and Events

Vancouver celebrates the arts with major international festivals. Summer is particularly active, so make reservations in advance. Call (604) 683-2000 to request printed information, including a complete listing of events and dates; or visit <www.tourismvancouver.com>.

January–February: Chinese New Year Festival; Women in View Festival.

March: Vancouver Storytelling Festival; Pacific Rim Whale Festival; Celtic Fest and St Patrick's Day Parade.

April: Vancouver Playhouse International Wine Festival; World Ski and Snowboard Festival (Whistler); Eat! Vancouver, the Everything Food and Cooking Festival.

May: Vancouver International Children's Festival; New Music West international music festival; Adidas Vancouver International Marathon.

June: International Jazz Festival; Alcan Dragon Boat Festival; Vancouver Shakespeare Festival, Bard on the Beach; Vancouver Francophone Summer Fesival; Up in the Air Theatre Festival; B.C. Highland Games (Coquitlam); Stanley Park Bike Festival.

July: Canada Day at Canada Place; The 10-day Dancing on the Edge Festival; Vancouver Folk Music Festival; Caribbean Days Festival; Chamber Music Festival; Celebration of Light (fireworks); Sea Vancouver Festival; Early Music Festival; Molson Indy Vancouver.

August: Festival Vancouver; The Fair at the PNE; Out on Screen (gay and lesbian film festival); Gay Pride Parade; Pacific National Exhibition; Powell Street Festival; Cameo Music Festival.

September: Fringe Festival (theatre, comedy, dance, music, improv, etc.); Vancouver Film Festival; Vancouver Autumn Brewmasters' Festival.

October: Vancouver International Comedy Festival; Vancouver International Writers' and Readers' Festival; Vancouver International Film Festival; University of British Columbia Botanical Gardens Apple Festival.

November: North American Native Arts and Crafts Festival (Nov or Dec); Vancouver Storytelling Festival; Christmas at Hycroft.

December: Christmas Carol Ship Parade; Van Dusen Botanical Garden Festival of Lights; Whistler Film Festival (Whistler); Christmas at Canada Place; Bright Nights in Stanley Park.

EATING OUT

Vancouverites are known to be pretty modest about their city and its attributes, so most would probably hesitate to apply superlatives to Vancouver's restaurants. Given the relatively recent emergence of Vancouver as a destination, how could its food possibly rank with that of such culinary centres as San Francisco, Chicago and New York?

Those in the know might forcefully counter that Vancouver is already a player on the world food scene. But everyone would agree that there have been momentous, welcome changes in the restaurant industry. It wasn't so long ago that dining out in Vancouver meant Chinese or Italian or Greek food from menus that hadn't veered off course from the day the restaurants opened. Special-occasion meals called for

Outdoor dining in Granville

reservations at the steak house. While some of those establishments are still thriving, the idea of what it means to eat out has shifted recently in the minds of many. Going out to dinner is now as much about having a total experience – the food,

> **West Coast fish and shellfish is superlative, from the succulent Alaskan king crabs to salmon from local rivers, and the fine chefs of Vancouver know exactly what to do with it.**

the wine, the atmosphere – as it is about filling your stomach. Perhaps more so. And an ever-growing number of chefs are guiding the way with innovative, seasonal and artistic dishes that reflect a great passion for food and presentation.

That's not to say dining out in Vancouver has become stuffy or pretentious. Vancouver is happy with its reputation as a laid-back city where 'smart-casual' is about as dressy as you need to get. The staff in the majority of restaurants, no matter how renowned the reputation, are refreshingly free of attitude. And the diners themselves demand value. Vancouverites aren't particularly anxious to throw their dollars about, but they do like to eat out as often as possible. Since restaurants must rely on a local following to get them through the long winters, it's becoming increasingly easier to get a great meal at a reasonable price.

Healthy Eating

Vancouver's general ambiance also drives the food scene. The health-conscious locals prefer light, flavourful dishes, and chefs are a step ahead, substituting essences of stocks and broths for heavy sauces and making a huge demand on Fraser Valley farmers for innovative greens and organic fruits and produce throughout the year. British Columbia's bountiful seafood provides the basis for everything from a simple salmon steak to grilled scallops wrapped in bacon to

Daily catch

raw shellfish bars that bring tears to the eyes of otherwise toughened oyster zealots. Vancouver's multiculturalism has also played a major role in the food revolution. Pacific Northwest meets Pacific Rim and the resulting fusion frequently marries ingredients that don't necessarily speak the same language but know how to have a good time on Italian-pottery plates. It is a happy marriage indeed.

When and Where to Eat

In general, Vancouver hotels do not include breakfast in the price of a room, though a few provide a Continental breakfast. However, you'll find plenty of cafés, coffee shops and bakeries where you can get a bite to tide you over until lunch. Some eateries serve breakfast all day, or at least until 2 or 3pm. A fancy 'brunch' is always available at the bigger hotels, but you can also create your own late-morning meal while shopping at such emporia as the Granville Public Market. Watching locals sampling the fare while strolling through the city's shopping districts is the best way to discover what Vancouverites eat for lunch, and your choices here are as varied as the city's neighbourhoods.

When it comes to the evening meal, this isn't Barcelona. The locals are buttering their bread by 7 or 8pm and kitchens begin closing at 10pm, although you'll find a few open until 11. Once you decide what time you'll be ready for dinner, the more difficult question to answer is where to eat.

Fine Dining

If you're interested in sampling the best of what Vancouver offers in fine dining, your choices are vast. While locals don't usually scamper to eat at hotel restaurants, many of these kitchens are producing outstanding dishes. In particular, **Diva at the Met** has been getting lots of attention from

---

Wild About Salmon

Salmon is the reigning king of the waters in British Columbia, first revered by Coast Salish people who survived on the abundant fish. Salmon was even the province's major export for a short period of time in the 1800s, prior to the completion of the railway. The Fraser River still provides two-thirds of the area's total sockeye catch, but other salmon, particularly coho, have suffered from over-fishing and habitat destruction.

There are five different types of salmon. Chinook (or king) salmon is the largest of them all, with firm ivory to deep-red flesh. Commercial harvests are small. Chum salmon flesh ranges from pale to medium red and is often canned under the name of keta salmon. Coho salmon, a popular, moderately priced variety is no longer readily available due to its status as a threatened species. Sockeye salmon is the mainstay of the commercial fishing industry, with a firm, deep-red flesh. Pink salmon is the smallest of the lot and is usually canned.

Restaurants in B.C. seldom omit salmon – wild or farmed, local or imported – from the menu. Fresh wild salmon is available seasonally from June to September. Farmed salmon, much of which comes from the waters off Vancouver Island, is always available. According to some gourmets, they taste different, but you can decide for yourself.

To see and learn more about salmon, visit Capilano Park's fish hatchery (4500 Capilano Park Road, tel: 604/666-1790) in North Vancouver. Breeding tanks, a glass-fronted observation deck, and displays combine to show and tell their fascinating life-cycle.

Haute cuisine, Vancouver-style

the 'Best of' lists, but there are many others that offer exceptional food and service. Of the many locally owned upmarket eateries, **Bishop's** is always on the tip of every gourmet's tongue. Many chefs received their start in the kitchen of this West 4th Avenue institution, and John Bishop can be personally credited with spicing up the city's culinary stew. To get unbiased advice on restaurants outside the listings in the back of this book, turn to *City Foods* or the weekly *Georgia Straight*, free publications that you can pick up in city bookstores and cafés.

Neighbourhood Restaurants

Handsome neighbourhood restaurants are always cropping up, offering comforting menus at affordable prices to keep the regulars happy and the tourists elated. This welcome trend is best exemplified by intimate spaces such as **LilyKate**, on Hamitton Street. It won't take a great deal of trouble to find the gems, so ask around for recommendations, make reservations, and never settle for what's convenient or for any place where the food is secondary to a theme or a T-shirt. Even if you come from a place where great meals are commonplace, Vancouver chefs are sure to delight your palate.

Ethnic Vancouver

Multiculturalism adds immeasurably to a city, especially when it's time to eat. In Vancouver, it's a certainty that adventurous, curious or merely gung-ho eaters won't be disappointed with the range of food available. You'll easily find French, Italian, Greek, Chinese and, of course, American-style restaurants, but with a little further investigation you can also discover Hungarian, Japanese, Indian, Korean, Southeast Asian, Mexican and even Native American eateries. So if you need to redirect a debate on where to eat, decide instead what type of food you'd like to try.

Excellent Chinese restaurants abound, with some of the finest located in the nearby suburb of Richmond. For Indian food, **Vij's** is the last word.

Casual Dining

If you're satisfied with a Continental breakfast, you'll find freshly baked goods and coffee on practically every street corner. Otherwise, you can fill up for a long day of sightseeing at **Sophie's Cosmic Café** on West 4th Avenue. Along Robson Street and Denman Street there are many pavement cafés and casual restaurants serving lunch and dinner. The **Public Market** on Granville Island is another wonderful place to find breakfast, lunch, snacks, baked goods and deli items. You'll always have better luck finding reasonably priced places to eat outside the downtown business district. Try Commercial Drive for Italian food,

Health-conscious and hungry? No problem in Vancouver

West Broadway for Greek fare, and West 4th Avenue for vegetarian choices.

Drinking

Vancouver is a sociable place, where the downtown population like to get out after work, chill out with a glass of B.C. wine or a beer from one of the many local microbreweries. Outside the restaurants, bars and pubs, however, alcohol sales are strictly controlled (and highly taxed) by the British Columbia Liquor Distribution Branch (BCLDB), so purchasing wine, beer or spirits isn't as straightforward as walking into a corner convenience store. There are a few private wine shops and some beer and wine outlets connected to pubs, but if you wish to buy alcohol, you'll need to find a BCLDB store. Downtown, there's one at 1120 Alberni Street. Call the BCLDB wine line (tel: 604/660-9463) for hours and information. For wine only, try the private Marquis Wine Cellars downtown (1034 Davie Street) or the Broadway International Wine Shop (2752 West Broadway).

The Word on Wine

Vancouverites are statistically the highest per-capita consumers of wine in any North American city. Many restaurants pride themselves on their cellars, featuring bottles from every wine-growing region in the world, including the province's own renowned Okanagan Valley and perhaps even from less famous, but burgeoning Vancouver Island wineries. Wine is heavily taxed and relatively expensive in Canada, though.

Beers and Breweries

Beer is not native to Vancouver, but based on its importance to the population it ranks right up there with sunny days and the Canucks hockey team. Two breweries, the Red Cross Brewing Company and the Vancouver Brewery, opened here in 1882. Through mergers and acquisitions these original companies disappeared, but microbreweries have spread throughout the province.

Due to rather complicated Canadian alcohol laws, you can only purchase beer from the manufacturer if it operates a brew-pub: where the beer is both made and imbibed. Popular local brew-pubs include **Yaletown Brewing** at 1111 Mainland in Yaletown; **Steamworks BrewPub** at 375 Water Street in Gastown; and, in North Vancouver, **Sailor Hägar's BrewPub** at 375 Semisch Avenue. It's also possible to tour some regular breweries, but to sample their wares you'd

The majority of restaurants are licensed to serve alcohol, but it's a good idea to check first. The legal age for drinking in Canada is 18 or 19, depending on the state; in B.C. it is 19.

have to go elsewhere. One local brewery that offers tours is **Granville Island Brewing Company** (tel: 604/687-2739).

Crazy for Caffeine

Walking down busy Robson Street, you will eventually be confronted with the vision of two Starbucks coffee shops holding down opposite corners. You aren't seeing double. This is merely one indication that you've arrived in a city that's utterly devoted to caffeine. Whether this is due to its proximity to Seattle (the home of Starbucks); the inroads being made by Canadian chain,

Coffee break

Tim Horton's; or to the high number of rainy days isn't clear, but coffee reigns supreme and coffee bars can be found in bookstores, laundromats, office buildings, strip malls and just about anywhere else where there's an electrical outlet for the cappuccino maker.

Perplexed by the lingo? 'A double half-and-half, lowfat, no-foam latte, please' is just the easy way to request two shots of espresso, one decaffeinated and one regular, with steamed 2 percent milk but without the foam on top. Tell the barista what you want and they will make it for you, with or without the fancy lingo. You may also notice jars gracing the counters of coffeehouses that do not provide table service. If you feel the urge, drop your change in there as a tip.

HANDY TRAVEL TIPS

An A–Z Summary of Practical Information

A Accommodation   104
Airports 105
B Bicycle Hire . . . 106
Budgeting for
Your Trip 106
C Camping 108
Car Hire 108
Climate 109
Clothing 109
Crime and Safety 109
Customs and Entry
Requirements . 110
D Driving 110
E Electricity 112
Embassies and
Consulates . . . 112
Emergencies . . . 112
G Gay and Lesbian
Travellers   112
Getting There . . . 113
Guided Tours . . .114
H Health and
Medical Care . 115
Hitchhiking 115

L Language 116
Laundry and
Dry Cleaning . 116
Legal Holidays . . 116
M Maps 116
Media 117
Money 117
O Opening Hours . 119
P Police 119
Post Offices 119
Public Transport . 120
R Religious Services 121
S Smoking 121
T Telephones 122
Tickets 122
Time Zones 123
Tipping 123
Toilets 123
Tourist
Information   . . 124
W Websites 124
Weights and
Measures 125
Y Youth Hostels . . 125

A

ACCOMMODATION

'Gassy' Jack Deighton opened the first saloon in Gastown in 1867, but the taxman soon appeared at his door telling him to either operate a hotel or lose his alcohol permit. He opened Deighton House in 1870, and although it was destroyed in the Great Fire of 1886, along with nearly every other building in the town, the hospitality business already had a firm foothold in what soon became Vancouver. By the following year the first Hotel Vancouver had opened, and the city has seen a steady rise in room numbers ever since.

Today, a number of new hotels are under construction, while many of the older properties have had a facelift or are in the process of renovation. Even when they are enjoying high occupancy rates, the far-sighted hoteliers of Vancouver don't coast on their reputations.

Depending on your budget, options range from basic motor lodges to luxurious A A A five-diamond properties featuring knowledgeable concierges, a courtesy limousine service and splendid health spas. While it can be rewarding to explore some of the more off-the-beaten-track locations for lodging, such as the North Shore, the majority of rooms are located downtown, convenient for every part of the metropolitan area by public transport, private car or taxi and within walking distance of many attractions. Downtown hotels tend to be fairly large (better for attracting convention business), although the industry is slowly jumping on the boutique hotel bandwagon.

There are a handful of small hotels downtown and a fair number of B&Bs in other neighbourhoods for those who prefer more intimate digs. To obtain a list of inns and bed-and-breakfasts, contact British Columbia Tourism (tel: 800/435-5622; <www.hellobc.com>). For the truly budget-minded, the University of B.C. (tel: 604/822-1000) lets student housing during the summer, with a few units available during the school year, and Hostelling International have a place in the West End (tel: 604/584-4565 or 1-888/203-4302).

It is highly recommended to reserve rooms in advance, especially during the summer when you will be competing with the endless stream of cruise ships that port here on their way to Alaska. Rates are at their highest from April to October, with July and August commanding top dollar, particularly in resorts on the outlying islands. Vancouver is a popular convention city, so the big hotels can also be booked up during the least likely times. Vancouver Central Reservations (tel: 1-888/895-2870 or 604/904-7080; from the UK tel: 0880/731-6387) will help. Hotel taxes add another 17 percent to your bill: 10 percent for the provincial hotel and motel room sales tax, and 7 percent for the GST, which is refundable if you send in your receipt and a refund form, available at your hotel (see MONEY MATTERS below). If you have a car, hotel parking costs from $7 to $18 a day.

AIRPORTS

Vancouver International Airport is located in the suburb of Richmond, about a 20-minute drive from downtown Vancouver. Expanded in 1996, it now sports a new international terminal that leads passengers in smooth succession through Canadian customs to the baggage claim area. The original terminal now serves as the gateway to flights within Canada. All the major car rental companies are just steps away from the exit doors, making pick-up and drop-off particularly easy and very efficient. Taxis are also readily available and cost approximately $21 to downtown sites; you'll pay a bit more during rush hour because of the extra time it takes. The green Airporter bus ($10 one-way, $17 round trip) provides an alternative, and picks up outside the baggage claim area, but it stops at virtually every downtown hotel, creating an interminable ride if you happen to be staying somewhere near the end of the bus loop. Unless you are travelling on your own and on a tight budget, it's really not worth inconveniencing yourself.

When you leave Vancouver, if you haven't quite finished shopping, it's good to know that the airport shops charge the same prices that you'd pay in town.

B

BICYCLE HIRE

Cycling around the Stanley Park seawall will make you feel like one of the locals you'll meet along the way. There are also many kilometres of trails into the heart of the park, and the seawall links up with the 15-km (9½-mile) Vancouver Seaside Bicycle Route at the southern end of the park. You can also take your wheels over to Granville Island on designated AquaBus routes.

Enquire if your hotel has bikes to loan; otherwise, you can hire bicycles and/or roller blades along Denman Street at any of several shops between Georgia and Alberni. For complete information on bike paths, pick up a free *Cycling in Vancouver* map at bike shops, libraries, and community centres; on the Internet check out <www.city.vancouver.bc.ca/engsvcs/transport/cycling/bikepage>. In Steveston, there are 10km (6 miles) of cycle and walking paths along the dykes around Garry Point Park. Remember that helmets are a legal requirement for cyclists.

Mountain-bike enthusiasts should head out of the city to Squamish, at the head of Howe Sound, where rentals are available for use on the world-class trails.

BUDGETING FOR YOUR TRIP

Vancouver isn't an inexpensive destination, even during the low season, but much also depends on the current value of the Canadian dollar in relation to your country's currency. Travellers from the US have been enjoying highly favourable rates recently, transforming fancy $200 hotel rooms into $130 bargains. When budgeting, decide how much you can afford to spend, divide it by the number of days you'll be on holiday, then plan your lodging and meal choices to accommodate your finances (and add another 20 percent for contingencies). If you are flexible and can travel in late autumn or winter, you'll save on admission fees at most attractions and get great hotel deals.

Accommodation. Expect to pay from $75 for a small double at a plain hotel like the extremely popular Sylvia to $360 for an executive double at a luxury hotel such as the Wedgewood. Don't forget that taxes are not included in the quoted rooms rates; you'll need to add 17 percent for this, plus about $15 per day for parking. The 10 percent G S T payback will be a bonus after you get home again, but it can take a while to come through, so don't include it in your calculations.

Meals. Vancouverites are becoming sensitive to price when it comes to dining out, and many eateries are responding to the pressure to keep the cost at a reasonable level. In general, entrées at the better restaurants start at around $16 à la carte and can easily reach $28 or more. Ethnic restaurants are usually quite a bit less expensive, as are restaurants outside the central business district. Portions are generous nearly everywhere you go. If you want to have a bottle of wine with your meal, you probably won't find much on the wine list priced at less than $20.

Transport. Buses arrive frequently on most street corners and cost $2.25 (exact change required) one-way in town, a little more to the outlying areas. A taxi fare from downtown to Kitsilano will cost around $10. The short hop on the AquaBus from Hornby to Granville Island is $2.50. If you have a car, plan to pay for parking wherever you go: most pay parking takes credit cards and the charge is $2–$6 per hour. Street parking requires change for the meters, except in residential districts. Ferries to Vancouver Island cost about $50 if you are taking a car, plus another $12 per person. Hire cars *(see below)* will add another $250 or more per week, not including the fuel.

Attractions. You'll generally be paying from $7 for the U B C Museum of Anthropology to about $25 to walk around Victoria's Butchart Gardens, but the anthropology museum is free on Tuesdays from 5–8pm, and you can find other free or low-cost things to see, including Capilano Salmon Hatchery, Lynn Canyon Park and Seymour Conservation Park. Tourist Information Centres will have information.

C

CAMPING

Camping is a great way to appreciate the wonderful landscapes that surround Vancouver, and there are plentiful campsites all kinds, from remote, hike-in-only sites for backpackers in the national and provincial parks to fully serviced places for RVs (motorhomes) and tents, with electric hook-ups, cable and telephone points, and lots of leisure amenities. One such park in the greater Vancouver area is the Burnaby Cariboo RV Park (tel: 604/420-1722; <www.bcrv.com>).

Should you wish to camp in a provincial park or in the Pacific Rim National Park Reserve on Vancouver Island, you'll need to make reservations (tel: 604/689-9025 or toll-free in North America 800/689-9025; <www.discovercamping.ca>; for the West Coast Trail in the Pacific Rim National Park Reserve: 250/387-1642 or toll-free in North America 800/435-5622).

CAR HIRE

Public transport in and around Vancouver is quite good (if crowded) and driving can be hectic in the city. Add the parking charges (including hotel parking) and you may feel a car is unneccessary for a city-based stay. However, it's much more convenient to have your own wheels for out-of-town trips, so you might want to hire one on an as-needed basis. It does pay to compare prices among companies; you can do so easily on the Internet and even make your reservations online. Drivers must be over 25 years old, carry a valid Canadian, US or International Driver's Licence, and have a credit card. Optional damage waivers increase the cost, so check with your own insurer whether your regular coverage also includes rentals. Avis, Budget, Hertz and Thrifty all operate on the airport premises, with more companies in town. A small car with automatic transmission will cost around $30 to $40 a day plus hefty taxes, and there'll be airport fees too if you hire from an airport branch.

CLIMATE

Vancouver enjoys a temperate climate and a reputation for rain. Summers can be quite lovely and you might even see people wearing T-shirts and shorts in October, although in the evenings you'll always want a jacket. British Columbia is the only province in Canada where average winter temperatures remain above freezing, and though you can expect precipitation, there'll be no snow in the city proper. However, the topography does affect the weather, and the Coast and Rocky Mountains provide superb conditions for winter sports within a couple of hours drive of the snow-free city.

Average daily temperatures are: July/August: 22–23°C (72–73°F); December/January: 6°C (43°F); spring and autumn: 14–18°C (57–63°F)

CLOTHING

This is a casual city, where exercise clothes take up the most space in people's wardrobes. Unless you hope to impress the fit young things shooting pool in Yaletown or lining up outside certain clubs, don't worry too much about your wardrobe. Pack walking shoes, a light raincoat and smart/casual clothes (if you plan to haunt the better restaurants). For the beaches (except naturist Wreck Beach) and hotel pools, you will also want a swimsuit. If you will be travelling in the late autumn or winter, warm gloves, a hat and a coat will keep you happy. You might need an umbrella at any time of year.

CRIME AND SAFETY

Due in part to strict gun-control laws, Vancouver is quite safe, even at night, in nearly every neighbourhood. The majority of crimes are property related, so be sensible and don't leave valuables in your car. The diciest area for tourists is East Hastings Street between Chinatown and Gastown. These blocks are of great concern to the tourism industry, which is pushing City Hall to do something – exactly what, however, isn't clear. If you are on foot and want to walk from Gastown to Chinatown, take Carrall to East Pender. You'll still be asked for money, but not to any great extent. For a big city, there aren't the huge numbers of street people that you see elsewhere; most appear on Robson Street where the number of passers-by is the greatest. Police patrol on bikes and are easy to spot. In case of emergency, calling 911 will summon the police, an ambulance or the fire department.

CUSTOMS AND ENTRY REQUIREMENTS

Visitors from the US require a birth certificate or some other evidence of citizenship (such as a passport) to cross the border. Visitors from Australia, France, Ireland, New Zealand, and the United Kingdom need a valid passport. A visa is not necessary. Tourists travelling from South Africa will need a valid passport and a visa. You'll receive a customs declaration on the plane to complete and present on your way through the airport.

Children under 16 years who are not travelling with both of their parents must have written authorisation, signed before a notary, from the absent parent(s) or guardian.

Anyone with a criminal record (and this may include some driving offences, such as drink-driving), should contact the Canadian Embassy in their home country before travelling.

There are restrictions in the amounts of tobacco and alcohol visitors can bring into the country. For more specific rules, including banned items, contact the Canada Customs Office (tel: 604/666-0545; <www.ccra-adrc.gc.ca/customs>).

D

DRIVING

Downtown Vancouver is laid out in a grid pattern, so it's fairly simple to find your way around. Three bridges – Burrard, Granville and Cambie – cross False Creek to the rest of Vancouver's neighbourhoods to the south. To reach North and West Vancouver, head north on West Georgia Street through Stanley Park and over the Lions Gate (First

Narrows) Bridge. The direction cars take on the centre lane on West Georgia as it approaches the park changes depending on traffic patterns, so watch the signals. Head in the opposite direction on West Georgia over the viaduct to reach Vancouver's East Side and Commercial Drive.

Road conditions. Roads are well-maintained, though signage is sporadic.

Rules and regulations. Cars are driven on the right-hand side of the road, signs indicate local speed limits in kilometres per hour, and the wearing of seat belts, both back and front, is mandatory. It is permissable to turn right at a red light if there is no traffic from the left, but you must first come to a complete stop at the intersection. At crossroads without traffic lights in built-up areas, the first car to arrive gets priority; if two cars arrive at the same time, the one on the right gets to go first. Do not drive past a stationary yellow school bus with its hazard lights flashing from any direction.

Speed limits. Within urban areas the speed limit is between 40 and 60kmp (25 and 37mph); on rural roads it's 80kmp (50mph); on major roads it's 90kph (56mph) and on expressways 100kmp (62mph).

Fuel costs. Fuel is sold by the litre (about 83–99 cents a litre for regular), and filling stations are numerous.

If you need help. If you are a member of an automobile association in your home country, check for reciprocal membership with the B C A A (tel: 604/293-2222). If you are driving a hire car, the paperwork should include advice on what to do in the event of a breakdown. If you break down, raise the vehicle's bonnet (hood) to show you need assistance.

Parking. There's lots of competition for metered street parking everywhere you go, but there are also a fair number of parking garages in all the major shopping districts. Weighing up the cost of parking against public transport, it's often better to take the bus or train for trips downtown. Hotels maintain garages, for which you'll be charged between $5 and $17 per day. The less expensive the hotel, the cheaper the parking, and some do provide free parking.

E

ELECTRICITY

Canada uses 110 or 120 volts A C (60Hz), as in the US. Sockets take two-prong flat-pin plugs. The better hotels provide portable hair dryers, but if you are bringing electrical appliances from overseas, you'll need an adapter, and perhaps a voltage transformer (laptop computers are usually dual voltage, but still need an adaptor to plug in).

EMBASSIES AND CONSULATES

Consul of Australia	1228-888 Dunsmuir Street Tel: 604/684-1177
British Consulate General	800-1111 Melville Street Tel: 604/683-4421
French Consulate General	1100-1130 West Pender Street Tel: 604/681-4345
Consulate of Ireland	1400-100 West Pender Street Tel: 604/683-9233
United States Consulate	1095 West Pender Street Tel: 604/685-4311
New Zealand Consulate	1200-888 Dunsmuir Street Tel: 604/684-7388

EMERGENCIES

Dial 911 for police, fire or ambulance services. However, if you are on Vancouver Island you need to dial 0 and tell the operator you have an emergency. If you are in your hotel, call the switchboard.

G

GAY AND LESBIAN TRAVELLERS

Vancouver is a highly tolerant community, and gay and lesbian visitors will feel perfectly comfortable. The West End of Vancouver (not to be confused with West Vancouver across the Burrard Inlet) has a large gay population. For information on events or entertainment geared towards the gay community, contact the Gay and Lesbian Centre (tel: 604/684-5307). A weekly community magazine, *Xtr West,* publishes articles and entertainment listings of interest and there's lots of information, including what's on, gay-friendly business directory and a chatline on the website <www.gayvancouver.net>.

GETTING THERE (see also AIRPORTS)

By Air. Vancouver International Airport, Canada's gateway to Asia and the Pacific, is served by dozens of airlines, including Air New Zealand, British Airways, KLM, Lufthansa, and all the major US carriers. Over the Pacific, Air New Zealand flies from Auckland to Vancouver with one or two stops but no change of plane; Qantas offers a flight from Sydney with a change of plane in Honolulu; and United Airlines flies from Sydney to Vancouver with a stopover in San Francisco. There are direct flights from Europe departing from London, Amsterdam and Frankfurt. European travellers can also make connections through New York, Dallas, San Francisco and other US hubs.

A helicopter service is available to Victoria through Helijet Airways (tel: 1-800/665-4354 or 604/273-1414), as is a seaplane service through Harbour Air seaplanes (tel: 604/688-1277). This is the fastest, but most costly method of getting to Vancouver Island. Air Canada (tel: 1-888/247-2262) also operates a regular service.

By Rail. It's still possible to travel across the continent on the train route that brought Vancouver its early prosperity. It's one of the most spectacular trips in the world and a great way to see the country if time allows. As an example, the trip from Toronto takes just over three days (from about $420–$1,400 per person, depending on type of accommodation) and passes through northern Ontario, the Prairies and the Rocky Mountains before reaching the coast. For information, contact VIA Rail Canada (tel: 1-888/842-7245; <www.viarail.ca>).

By Car. The US border is only one hour's drive from Vancouver, and it takes about 2½ hours to drive to Vancouver from Seattle via Interstate 5 to Peace Arch/Blaine, then Highway 99 to Vancouver. TransCanada Highway 1 brings travellers into Vancouver from the east. Bring your passport.

By Sea. You don't really travel to Vancouver by sea – unless, that is, you are starting out from Vancouver Island or Prince Rupert up in northern British Columbia. However, Vancouver is a popular port on the Alaska cruise-ship route, hosting several big luxury liners a week between May and October, and passengers can tag on a stay in Vancouver at the beginning or end of their cruise. Ships dock downtown at the Canada Place Cruise Ship Terminal or at the Ballantyne Terminal, 5 minutes east of downtown.

GUIDED TOURS

Guided bus tours are great for an overview, but they usually don't give visitors a chance to discover much other than tourist attractions. And the city of Vancouver is best enjoyed on foot, not confined to a bus. Victoria, however is a different matter. If you don't plan to drive or fly there, a bus tour is the most cost-effective option. Gray Line (tel: 604/879-3363 or toll-free 800/667-0882) and Pacific Coach Lines (tel: 604/662-8074 or toll-free 800/661-1725) are two of the major operators.

Walking Tours. 'Gassy' Jack's statue at Water and Carrall streets in Gastown is the meeting place for a free 90-minute guided walking tour of Vancouver's oldest neighbourhood. Tour starts at 2pm daily (summer only), rain or shine. Tel: 604/683-5650 for information.

Boat Tours. To see the city at its best, you'll need to spend some time on the water. The SeaBus and Aquabus offer great views on their scheduled routes, but you can get proper tours with a commentary, too. Many of the boat charter companies are located in Coal Harbour. One outfit, Harbour Cruises, Ltd. (tel: 1-800-663-1500 or 604/688-7246), offers lunch and sunset dinner cruises, harbour tours and excursions up the coast and into beautiful Howe Sound, departing from the foot of Denman Street. You can also charter a smaller vessel for a more personal tour from Vancouver Boat Tours (tel: 604/261-6263; <www.vancouverboattours.com>).

H

HEALTH AND MEDICAL CARE

Hospitals. There are hospitals all around Vancouver for urgent medical care. St Paul's is downtown at 1081 Burrard Street (tel: 604/682-2344), with a 24-hour emergency room. Hospitals will not bill insurance companies, so be prepared to pay with cash or a credit card for treatment and obtain all the documentation you will need to make a claim afterwards; a visit will cost around $300.

Dentists. If you need dental treatment, ask your hotel to recommend a dentist, or consult the telephone directory. When you organise your travel insurance, make sure dental treatment is covered.

Drugstores (Pharmacies). For over-the-counter drugs, there are plenty of drugstore/pharmacies, including two on Robson Street, one in the Pacific Centre Mall on West Georgia and the 24-hour Shoppers' Drug Mart at 1125 Davie Street. Certain drugs require a doctor's prescription, so ask the pharmacist if you don't find what you are looking for on the shelves. If you are on regular prescription medication, make sure you bring enough from home to last for the duration of your stay and, as an extra precaution, bring a copy of your prescription.

Drinking water. If you are planning to do any backwoods camping, where you have to rely on spring water for drinking, you should make sure it is boiled for at least 10 minutes. Tap water is, of course, safe.

HITCHHIKING

It is illegal to pick up hitchhikers in British Columbia or to hitchhike on freeways. It is especially unwise for women to hitchhike, as prostitutes use this method to solicit business.

L

LANGUAGE

English is the primary language spoken in Vancouver. Mandarin and Cantonese are the languages of choice in the suburb of Richmond.

LAUNDRY AND DRY CLEANING

Most hotels provide same-day laundry and dry-cleaning services, but at a premium price. Your hotel desk clerk will be able to direct you to a self-service laundromat or dry-cleaner.

LEGAL HOLIDAYS

Banks, businesses and government offices are closed on these major Canadian holidays.

New Year's Day	1 January
Good Friday	Date varies in the spring
Easter Monday	Follows Good Friday
Victoria Day	Third Monday in May
Canada Day	1 July
British Columbia Day	First Monday in August
Labour Day	First Monday in September
Thanksgiving Day	Second Monday in October
Remembrance Day	11 November
Christmas Day	25 December
Boxing Day	26 December

M

MAPS

Your hotel concierge or desk clerk will give you a basic map of the city upon request. More detailed maps can be purchased at Vancouver Tourism Information Centre (200 Burrard Street, tel: 604/683-2000) and at the B.C. Automobile Association (999 West Broadway).

MEDIA

In print. For the best local entertainment listings, pick up a free copy of the *Georgia Straight* at your hotel, in many restaurants, and in bookstores; it is published every Thursday. The Vancouver edition of *Where* magazine also features listings. For informative articles on the region and its culture, check out *Vancouver Magazine* or its web-site: <www.vanmag.com>. Vancouver has two major daily news-papers: *The Vancouver Sun* and *The Province*. Canada's two national newspapers are *The National Post* and *The Globe and Mail*. Any of these can be purchased from pavement coin boxes, newsstands, or your hotel. International newspapers can be found at Mayfair News in the Royal Centre mall at Burrard and Georgia streets.

Television. Check the local papers for programme listings. Many channels that are available in Vancouver actually broadcast from Washington State in the US. If you are interested in watching local programmes, click channels 3 (Vancouver CBC), 4 (Community TV), and 13 (CKVU Vancouver).

Radio. There are many AM and FM stations in Vancouver. For local news tune to AM690 or AM980.

MONEY MATTERS

Currency. Canadian currency is based on dollars and cents. One-dol-lar coins are called 'loonies', after the bird pictured on the front, and, inevitably, two-dollar coins soon became known as 'twonies'. There are 100 cents in a dollar. The five-cent coin is known as a 'nickel', and 25 cents is a 'quarter'.

Currency exchange. While US dollars are accepted at most business establishments, the exchange rate won't be as high as you'd get at a bank and may even be taken on a 'one-for-one' basis, which is a very bad deal. Banks located in the financial centre downtown charge a small fee to exchange American dollars, but banks outside the down-town corridor do not. For other foreign currency exchange, major downtown banks generally operate foreign currency departments.

Bank hours vary, but most are open Monday to Friday from 9am to 5pm. Other currency exchange offices include Citizens' Bank of Canada (815 West Hastings Street, open Mon–Fri 6am–5pm); Thomas Cook Foreign Exchange (777 Dunsmuir Street, open Mon–Sat 9am– 5pm); and Bank of America at the Vancouver International Airport (open daily 6.15am–8pm).

Credit cards. Major credit cards are accepted nearly everywhere and provide the best rate of exchange. You'll need a credit card to hire a car and make hotel reservations.

ATMs. ATMs are readily available, accept most US and European cards and are convenient for obtaining cash at all hours. Most are on the MasterCard (Cirrus) or Visa (Plus) systems, so if one doesn't work with your card, try another. Bear in mind that for the use of the machine you'll probably be charged a transaction service fee by your bank as well as by the local bank.

Travellers' cheques. Travellers' cheques are accepted as cash in most establishments, and change is given in cash, but you might be asked for identification.

Taxes. Provincial sales tax (PST) of seven percent is added to all purchases with the exception of books, magazines and some groceries. In addition, a G S T (goods and services tax) of seven percent is added to everything but groceries. Hotels tack on an extra 10 percent for an accommodation tax as well.

You can get the GST portion refunded as long as you spend a total of more than $200 on refundable items and the individual items cost $50 or more. Refundable items include goods that will be taken out of Canada and accommodation, but not car hire, restaurants or other services. Obtain a GST refund form from your hotel or any store. You will need to fill in the form and send it with your original receipts to Revenue Canada; you'll receive a refund cheque within four to six weeks. A few counters in the airport and shops around town advertise G S T refunds on the spot, but they charge 15 percent of the proceeds.

O

OPENING HOURS

Shops. Store hours vary depending on the season, but are generally open Monday through Saturday from 10am to 6pm and Sunday from noon to 6pm. Stores in shopping centres are often open until 9pm on Thursday, Friday and Saturday nights, and many shops on Robson Street close nearer to 10pm in the summer (perhaps 11pm near Christmas and during the January sales).

Government offices. Open Monday to Friday, 9am to 4.30pm.

Museums and tourist attractions. In July and August, most attractions are open seven days a week from 10am until 5pm or later. The rest of the year, some museums are closed one day during the week (usually Monday or Tuesday), and many are open late one evening per week for a reduced admission charge or even for free.

Restaurants. For the most part, Vancouverites don't eat fashionably late. Dinner is consumed at any time between 6.30pm and 9.30pm, but you can find places that serve food until midnight. The legal drinking age in British Columbia is 19.

Banks. Hours vary, but most are open Monday to Friday from 9am to 5pm, and some for limited hours on Saturday.

P

POLICE

For police, Highway Patrol, fire or ambulance service in an emergency, telephone 911. You'll find that the police are polite and helpful.

POST OFFICES

The main post office is located at 349 West Georgia Street, and it is open Monday to Friday from 8am to 5.30pm. You can purchase stamps and send letters and parcels from any post office. Some newsstands also sell stamps. Mailboxes Etc also offer mail, express courier and shipping services, plus copy and print services, and will send faxes and sell packing materials and office supplies. There are five branches in Vancouver, including one in the Sinclair Centre on West Hastings Street.

PUBLIC TRANSPORT

Buses. The bus system in Vancouver is quite comprehensive. The Translink system includes buses, the SkyTrain and the SeaBus to Lonsdale Quay. For routes and information, call 604/953-3333 or pick up a free timetable at any public library, information centre or terminal. Fares depend on the number of zones crossed. The basic fare is $2.25, but during rush hour (weekdays before 9.30am and weekday afternoons between 3 and 6.30pm) the fare for outlying zones increases to $3.25–$4.50. You will need exact change to buy a ticket on the bus, or you can get tickets and passes from retailers that display the blue-and-red 'Faredealer' sign or from machines at SkyTrain and SeaBus depots. Transfers or validated tickets are good for 90 minutes in any direction, on any part of the system; for example, your SeaBus ticket is also valid on the bus or SkyTrain within the designated time period.

SkyTrain. This partially elevated rapid transit system operates every three to five minutes and currently runs on two lines. If you don't have a car, you might use SkyTrain to get to Science World or for a short tour of the city. There are some good views, too.

SeaBus. These passenger-only ferries cross Burrard Inlet every 15 to 30 minutes during the day and are a scenic and inexpensive way to see the harbour. Connecting buses await at the Lonsdale Quay terminal.

AquaBus. Tiny motorised ferries ply False Creek from the Hornby Street dock to Granville Island, Yaletown, Stamp's Landing and Science World. Fares begin at $3 for adults and $1 for children.

BC Ferries. Operated by the Province of British Columbia, huge ferry boats accommodate buses, lorries, cars, bicycles and passengers on foot. They provide snack bars and video games, not to mention plenty of gorgeous scenery along the way. Schedules are available from your hotel concierge or desk clerk, at the ferry terminals and at tourist information centres *(see page 124)*. The ferries going to Vancouver Island (Victoria) depart from Tsawwassen, a 1½-hour drive from downtown Vancouver, for a1½-hour voyage that ends at Swartz Bay. Ferries also leave from Horseshoe Bay in West Vancouver and dock at Bowen Island, Langdale on the Sunshine Coast, and Departure Bay, near Nanaimo on central Vancouver Island. Passenger fares are based on distance, and are higher during the summer and at weekends. Major credit cards, travellers' cheques and cash are all accepted.

Taxis. Since the fares include GST and start at $2.75, taxis are an expensive method of transport. You can pick one up easily at any of the major hotels, or you can telephone one of several companies: Yellow Cab (tel: 604/681-1111), Vancouver Taxi (tel: 604/871-1111) or Black Top (tel: 604/731-1111).

R

RELIGIOUS SERVICES

Just about every religion is represented in Vancouver. For a listing of services, ask at your hotel or check the 'Churches' listing in the yellow pages of the local telephone directory for the number of your preferred place of worship.

S

SMOKING

Smoking is prohibited inside restaurants, bars and public buildings. It is currently only allowed in designated smoking areas, such as cigar lounges. Before lighting up in a taxi, ask the driver. The larger hotels have designated smoking floors. If the reservations agent forgets to ask if you prefer a smoking or non-smoking room, you should mention it if it makes a difference to you.

T

TELEPHONES

The area codes for the metropolitan Vancouver area are 604 and 778; for Vancouver Island and the rest of British Columbia, it is 250. To place a local call within the metropolitan Vancouver area, simply dial the 10-digit number, including the area code. To call outside the area, first dial 1, the area code, and then the seven-digit number. From outside North America, dial the international access code (001) first, then follow the instructions above. The major hotels and airlines have toll-free '1-800' numbers for reservations, but some are only toll-free within the US or Canada. You can still get through on the number from elsewhere, but will get a recorded message telling you that there will be a charge for the call and giving you the option to continue or hang up.

Pay phones are located on the street, inside restaurants and inside hotels. Local calls cost 25 cents. If you use a calling card, be advised that your long-distance carrier probably charges a premium for the privilege. Check beforehand to avoid surprises on your bill. If you phone from your hotel room, you will also be charged an extra fee, probably $1 per call, though some hotels offer free local calls.

TICKETS FOR EVENTS

For information on all the arts in Vancouver, call the Arts Hotline (tel: 604/684-2787; Mon–Sat 9am–5.30pm).

Ticketmaster. You can purchase tickets for events over the telephone or online with American Express, Visa or MasterCard through Ticketmaster (tel: 604/280-4444; <www.ticketmaster.ca>) or in person at the Ticketmaster outlet at 1304 Hornby Street.

Tickets Tonight. This agency, a partnership between Tourism Vancouver and the Alliance for Arts and Culture, covers the same events as Ticketmaster, plus many independent events and half-price tickets for same-day performances (subject to availability). The ticket booth is at the TouristInfo Centre (Plaza Level, 200 Burrard Street, tel: 604/684-2787; Tue–Sat 11am–6pm; <www.ticketstonight.ca>). Tickets can also be purchased direct from the venue, of course.

TIME ZONES

Vancouver, like the western United States, is in the Pacific Time Zone (GMT/UTC –7 hours). Daylight Savings Time (DST) is adopted in summer, and clocks are set forward by one hour at 2am on the first Sunday in April, and back an hour at 2am on the last Sunday in October.

TIPPING

In general, tipping is expected in restaurants, bars and taxis as well as for baggage handlers and tour guides. Unlike Britain, a tip is expected in a pub or bar even if you stand at the counter. The rule of thumb is 15 percent or up to 20 percent for exceptional service.

Waiters/waitresses	15 to 20 percent of the bill (before taxes)
Bartenders	$1 per round of drinks; more for a large crowd
Hotel/airline porters	$1 per bag
Hotel maid	$1 per day
Parking attendants	$1
Taxi drivers	15 percent
Tour guides	10 to 15 percent
Hairdressers/barbers	15 percent

TOILETS

Public toilets (ask for the washroom or bathroom) are readily available at filling stations, at tourist attractions and parks, and in hotels and restaurants, although in the last instance you may need to be a customer to use one. You won't find attendants in any of these places as a rule, but you should find that the facilities are very clean and well-maintained.

TOURIST INFORMATION OFFICES

Vancouver. Tourism Vancouver is a helpful source of information on Vancouver and the surrounding area. Before your trip, request a copy of their *Vancouver Book* – a magazine, actually – which contains a calendar of events, hotel and restaurant listings, and other useful information about the city. Their postal address is 200 Burrard Street, Suite 210, Vancouver, B.C. V6C 3LC, Canada (tel: toll-free in North America 1-800/663-6000 or 604/682-2222 locally). For information while you are in Vancouver, call in at the TouristInfo Centre, located at the Waterfront Centre (Plaza level) on Burrard Street (tel: 604/683-2000). Helpful staff are on hand to offer assistance, and there's also a Tickets Tonight booth *(see page 122)*. Tourism British Columbia also maintains an office in the UK, at 1 Regent Street, London, England SW1Y 4NS.

Victoria. For information about Victoria, write to Tourism Victoria, 710-1175 Douglas Street, Victoria, B.C. V8W 2E1, Canada. While you are in Victoria, you'll find the tourist information office across from the Empress Hotel on Government Street.

Whistler. For information about Whistler, write to the Whistler Resort Association, 4010 Whistler Way, Whistler, B.C. V0N 1B4, Canada. This is also the location of their Whistler Activity Centre, where you can get event tickets, restaurant recommendations, book tours and pick up maps and brochures.

WEBSITES

The web is useful for reading up on the city, making hire-car and airline reservations, and, in some cases, booking hotel rooms. The following websites are particularly well researched and up-to-date:

- <www.discovervancouver.com> Great design and content from the publisher of *The Greater Vancouver Book*, an urban encyclopedia.
- <www.tourismvancouver.com> Official city tourist site.
- <www.vancouver.com> Useful but very commercial.
- <www.vanmag.com> Site of *Vancouver Magazine*, with penetrating food and entertainment guides and regional articles.

• <www.translink.bc.ca> Site of the transport authority.
• <www.city.victoria.bc.ca> Victoria's official city site, with good links.
• <www.tourismwhistler.com> Official Tourism Whistler site – well designed, easy to use and with comprehensive information.
• <www.hellobc.com> British Columbia's official site and guide.
• <www.pc.gc.ca> Parks Canada Agency site, giving details of national parks, national historic sites and national marine conservation areas.
• <www.mytelus.com> Site produced by Telus is thorough, with Canadian stock quotes, and numerous listings, including phone.

W

WEIGHTS AND MEASURES

Canada uses the international metric system. For US travellers to Canada, some approximate equivalents are as follows: 1 US gallon is about 4 litres; 1 mile equals 1.6 kilometres; and 1 pound equals 0.45 kilograms. An easy way to translate temperature from Celsius to Fahrenheit is to multiply the degrees Celsius by 2 and add 30 (for example, 8°C = 46°F).

Y

YOUTH HOSTELS

If you are interested in staying at any of the many youth hostels around British Columbia, it's best to purchase an International Youth Hostel card before your arrival. All B.C. hostels belong to the International Youth Hostel Federation. In Vancouver, budget travellers can enjoy million-dollar views for $21.50 per night (non-members) in peak season at the Jericho Beach Hostelling International/Vancouver (1515 Discovery, tel: 1-888/203-4303). Hostelling International's downtown property (1114 Burnaby Street, tel: 1-888/203-4302) has recently been renovated and costs $24 per night (non-members). Consult their website at <www.hihostels.bc.ca> for other locations, including Victoria and Whistler.

Recommended Hotels

Vancouver developers are busily adding a few thousand rooms to accommodate the influx of travellers arriving year round. Once the dust settles, visitors may see a drop in the high-season room rates. Prices are steep between May and October. The slower autumn and winter months find Vancouver promoting attractive hotel packages that feature discounted rooms plus theatre tickets or dining deals.

In general, B.C. hoteliers maintain excellent standards of cleanliness and service. Rooms usually include cable TV, direct-dial phones and air conditioning, and if there is no concierge, the desk clerks will strive to provide directions and information. You must book in advance during the high season – the earlier the better. There are often discounts for Internet booking. For late reservations, call 1-800-HELLOBC (locally: 604/663-6000), or visit <www.hellobc.com>.

The price bands below refer to high-season rack rates (in Canadian dollars) for a standard double room, without breakfast or parking unless noted, and exclusive of taxes (15–17 percent). When making reservations at larger hotels, always ask about weekend packages, special promotions and discounts, even during the summer. A plus sign (+) means 'and up'.

$$$$$	above $250
$$$$	$200–$250
$$$	$150–$200
$$	$125–$150
$	below $125

STANLEY PARK

Coast Plaza Suite Hotel $$–$$$$$ *1763 Comox Street, Vancouver, B.C. V6G 1P6, tel: 604/688-7711, toll-free 1-800/663-1144, fax: 604/688-5934, <www.coasthotels.com>.* The views at this recently renovated West End high-rise hotel are lovely, especially from the rooms facing nearby Stanley Park. Located just off lively Denman Street. Spacious accommodation (the majority of which consists of suites), most with kitchens. Amenities include an indoor pool, saunas, exercise room, two restaurants and a nice low-key atmosphere. 269 rooms.

Sylvia Hotel $$$ *1154 Gilford Street, Vancouver, B.C. V6G 2P6, tel: 604/681-9321, fax: 604/682-3551, <www.sylviahotel.com>.* The dowdy Sylvia, housed in an historic eight-storey stone building just two blocks from Stanley Park, is one of the more sought-after addresses in the city. Yes, the rooms are plain, the bathrooms small and old-fashioned, and the lobby could stand a redo, but the location is superb and the price is right. Summer visitors should book a year in advance. 119 rooms.

Westin Bayshore $$$$$ *1601 Bayshore Drive, Vancouver, B.C. V6G 2V4, tel: 604/682-3377, toll-free 1-800/837-8461, fax: 604/687-3102, <www.westinbayshore.com>.* Corporate resort hotel overlooking Coal Harbour, with exquisite views. Has 26 meeting rooms, full health club (with massage therapist), indoor and outdoor pools and two restaurants. The location between Stanley Park and downtown is unbeatable. Wheelchair accessible. 510 rooms.

DOWNTOWN

Barclay Hotel $+ *1348 Robson Street, Vancouver, B.C. V6E 1C5, tel: 604/688-8850, fax: 604/688-2534, <www.barclayhotel.com>.* A budget hotel in a Heritage building featuring small rooms furnished with the basics. Location on busy Robson Street will appeal to walkers and people-watchers; balmy summer nights bring out the crowds, so expect a little noise. Restaurant and bar. 90 rooms.

Burrard Motor Inn $+ *1100 Burrard Street, Vancouver, B.C. V6Z 1Y7, tel: 604/681-2331, toll-free 1-800/663-0366, fax: 604/681-9753.* Pleasant three-storey motor inn in a good location, just two blocks from Robson Street. Rooms are simple and comfortable, some with kitchenettes, appropriate for visitors on a budget. Pleasant outdoor patio. Restaurant and lounge in hotel. Free parking. 71 rooms.

Comfort Inn Downtown $$–$$$+ *654 Nelson Street, Vancouver, B.C. V6B 6K4, tel: 604/605-4333, toll-free 1-888/605-5333, fax: 604/605-4334, <www.comfortinndowntown.com>.* Formerly the Hotel Dakota, this 1904 building was smartly renovated in 2001 into a trendy boutique hotel close to Yaletown and Granville Street cinemas. Small rooms are simply but sleekly furnished with '50s-style blond wood and black-and-white photos. Gay friendly. Two popular night spots: Fred's Uptown Tavern and the nightclub BaBalu, are connected. No views; reasonable parking fees. 82 rooms.

Fairmont Hotel Vancouver $$$$+ *900 West Georgia Street, Vancouver, B.C. V6C 2W6, tel: 604/684-3131, toll-free 1-800/441-1414, fax: 604/662-1929, <www.fairmont.com>.* Elegant, landmark chateau-style building that has recently been refurbished. Those who can tear themselves away from their well-appointed guest room can make a vacation out of wandering around the lobby and shopping arcade, splashing about in the spa and pool, or enjoying the hotel's two excellent restaurants. Wheelchair accessible. 556 rooms.

Fairmont Waterfront Centre $$$$$ *900 Canada Place Way, Vancouver, B.C. V6C 3L5, tel: 604/691-1991, toll-free 1-800/441-1414, fax: 604/691-1999, <www.fairmont.com/waterfront>.* This beautifully designed hotel at the harbour has glorious views. Rooms are large, delightfully decorated with French-country prints, and contain all the amenities one expects from a fancy business hotel, including a fitness centre and spa services. There is even a herb garden for guests to admire. Wheelchair accessible. 489 rooms.

Four Seasons $$$$$ *791 West Georgia Street, Vancouver, B.C. V6C 2T4, tel: 604/689-9333, toll-free 1-800/332-3442, fax: 604/684-4555.* Looming above the Pacific Centre mall this AAA five-diamond luxury hotel has a reputation for impeccable service. Health club, indoor/outdoor pool, 24-hour room service. The main restaurant (of three), Chartwells, is highly praised. 385 rooms including 91 suites.

Georgian Court Hotel $$$+ *773 Beatty Street, Vancouver, B.C. V6B 2M4, tel: 604/682-5555, toll-free 1-800/663-1155, fax: 604/682-8830, <www.georgiancourt.com>*. Intimate, upmarket hotel offers good value for the money. Rooms exude warmth and comfort. Fitness centre, four restaurants. Centrally located, close to Yaletown, B.C. Place and the Queen Elizabeth Theatre. Wheelchair accessible. 180 rooms.

Hotel Georgia $$$$ *801 West Georgia Street, Vancouver, B.C. V6C 1P7, tel: 604/682-5566, toll-free 1-800/633-1111*. The Crowne Plaza chain took over management of this 1927 property in 1998. Expensive renovation, with impressive lobby; bland rooms and baths are cell-like. Centrally located near downtown department stores. Fitness centre and popular dance club (Elements) on site. 312 rooms.

Howard Johnson Hotel $-$$$ *1176 Granville Street, Vancouver, B.C. V6Z 1L8, tel: 604/688-8701, toll-free 1-888/654-6336, fax: 604/688-8335, <www.hojovancouver.com>*. Formerly the Hotel Linden. The Howard Johnson chain recently assumed ownership of this newly renovated Heritage-style boutique hotel. Small-to-average guest rooms. Continental breakfast and complimentary use of fitness facilities across the street. Adjacent parking is only $8 per day. 110 rooms.

Hyatt Regency Vancouver $$$$-$$$$$ *655 Burrard Street, Vancouver, B.C. V6C 2R7, tel: 604/683-1234, toll-free 1-800/233-1234, fax: 604/639-4760, <www.vancouver.hyatt.com>*. Excellent service, lovely decor and a recent renovation, albeit with the generic Hyatt charm. Popular destination for tour groups and business travellers, it's good value considering the location. Standard guest rooms are large; for views, request an upper floor facing north. Fitness centre and outdoor pool. Wheelchair accessible. 644 rooms, 35 suites.

Listel **$$$$–$$$$$** *1300 Robson Street, Vancouver, B.C. V6E 1C5, tel: 604/684-8461, toll-free 1-800/663-5491, fax: 604/684-7092, <www.listel-vancouver.com>.* This hotel's subtle, stylish atmosphere contrasts sharply with all the activity outside on a busy stretch of Robson Street. There's original artwork in guest rooms on the two 'gallery' floors. Twice-daily maid service. Good restaurant with live jazz, indoor pool, gymnasium, whirlpool, valet parking. The special internet rates are worth checking out. Wheelchair accessible. 130 rooms.

Metropolitan Hotel **$$$$–$$$$$** *645 Howe Street, Vancouver, B.C. V6C 2Y9, tel: 604/687-1122, toll-free 1-800/667-2300, fax: 604/643-7267.* Across from the Pacific Centre underground mall. Tasteful and quiet, luxurious decor with modern Asian touches. Gracious rooms with cable TV. Swimming pool with a view, fitness centre, sauna, whirlpool, excellent restaurant (Diva at the Met). 197 rooms.

Pan Pacific **$$$$$** *300–999 Canada Place, Vancouver, B.C. V6C 3B5, tel: 604/662-8111, toll-free 1-800/937-1515, fax: 604/662-3815, <www.vancouver.panpacific.com>.* Triple-A five-diamond hotel at Vancouver's convention centre, with its famous five white 'sails' floating elegantly over the harbour. Guest rooms may be on the small side, but they make the most of the unparalleled setting, and all have luxurious amenities plus impeccable service. Health club, pool, services galore, car rental, and great views. 504 rooms.

Riviera Hotel **$–$$$** *1431 Robson Street, Vancouver, B.C. V6G 1C1, tel: 604/685-1301, toll-free 1-888/699-5222, fax: 604/685-1335, <www.rivieraonrobson.com>.* A converted apartment building on the west end of Robson. Good views. Most units have kitchenettes, free parking. 41 rooms.

Rosedale on Robson **$$$–$$$$$** *838 Hamilton Street, Vancouver, B.C. V6B 6A2, tel: 604/689-8033, toll-free 1-800/661-8870, fax: 604/689-4426, <www.rosedaleonrobson.com>.* All-suites hotel on a less frantic part of Robson Street offering the comforts of home. Helpful staff, a small playground, laundry facilities, exercise room, indoor pool, and a terrific location balance the ho-hum decor. A favourite with tour groups and airline personnel. Wheelchair accessible. 275 rooms. Major credit cards.

Sheraton Wall Centre $$$$–$$$$$ *1088 Burrard Street, Vancouver, B.C. V6Z 2R9, tel: 604/331-1000, toll-free 1-800/663-9255, fax: 604/893-7200.* Corporate travellers and tour groups make good use of this big (and getting bigger) glass-walled hotel. It's well-appointed, with large cheerful rooms, and the two-bedroom family suites make life on the road with children almost pleasant. The hotel is in a quiet location, yet is only a few blocks from boisterous Robson. Excellent concierge services. Wheelchair accessible. 733 rooms.

Sutton Place $$$$–$$$$$ *845 Burrard Street, Vancouver, B.C. V6Z 2K6, tel: 604/682-5511, toll-free 1-800/961-7555, fax: 604/682-5513, <www.suttonplace.com>.* A gracious and intimate AAA five-diamond hotel, with bright and spacious rooms and such amenities as thick terry-cloth bathrobes, loofahs and umbrellas. Twice-daily maid service, an excellent restaurant, European health spa, pool, and knowledgeable, friendly staff. Wheelchair accessible. 397 rooms.

Wedgewood Hotel $$$$$ *845 Hornby Street, Vancouver, B.C. V6Z 1V1, tel: 604/689-7777, toll-free 1-800/663-0666, fax: 604/608-5348, <www.wedgewoodhotel.com>.* Boutique hotel lavishly furnished with flowers, antiques and original art works. Prime location across from Robson Square and the Vancouver Art Museum. Twice-daily maid service, 24-hour room service, and an acclaimed restaurant (Bacchus). Wheelchair accessible. 83 rooms plus 34 suites.

GRANVILLE ISLAND

Granville Island Hotel $$$–$$$$ *1253 Johnston Street, Vancouver, B.C. V6H 3R9, tel: 604/683-7373, toll-free 1-800/663-1840, fax: 604/683-3061.* The unusual location on lively Granville Island provides nearly everything you could need – shopping, eateries, walking-distance attractions, and AquaBus transport. Nicely decorated rooms with hair dryers, irons and Internet access have marble floors and views. Restaurant, pub (with beer brewed on the premises) and lovely waterside patio, with wonderful views. Wheelchair accessible. 85 rooms.

NORTH VANCOUVER

Grouse Inn $–$$$$$ 1633 Capilano Road North, North Vancouver, B.C. V7P 3B3, tel: 604/988-7101, fax: 604/988-7102, <www.grouseinn.com>. Quality, two-storey motel in a great location on the north shore, set around a spacious area with parking, lawns, playground and a large heated pool. Rooms range from standard doubles to two-bedroom suites, Jacuzzi and honeymoon suites, all with cable TV and VCR, telephone, hair-dryer, iron, etc. Restaurant on site. Rates include a Continental breakfast. 80 rooms.

Lonsdale Quay $–$$$$$ *123 Carrie Cates Court, North Vancouver, B.C. V7M 3K7, tel: 604/986-6111, toll-free 1-800/836-6111, fax: 604/986-8782, <www.lonsdalequayhotel.com>.* For a different perspective on the city, travel across Burrard Inlet to this likeable little boutique hotel, on the waterfront above the Lonsdale Quay Public Market. The south-facing rooms have spectacular views of the city of Vancouver. Standard room amenities and transport options are great: the SeaBus whisks you to town in 15 enjoyable minutes. 70 rooms.

WEST VANCOUVER

Park Royal Hotel $$$ *540 Clyde Avenue, West Vancouver, B.C. V7T 2J7, tel: 604/926-5511, toll-free 1-877-926-5511, fax: 604/926-6082.* If you're interested in hiking or skiing Grouse Mountain or Cypress Park, or if you'd rather stay outside the city closer to Horseshoe Bay, this charming small hotel is warm and inviting. Although it's located next to a busy highway, the park-like grounds offer serenity, and rooms are cosy and attractively furnished. 30 rooms.

WHISTLER

The Whistler Resort Association will assist in making reservations in any of the 115 hotels, condos, and B&Bs in the area. The toll-free number is 1-800/944-7853; locally, call 604/664-5625.

Chateau Whistler (Fairmont) $$$$$ *4599 Chateau Boulevard, Whistler, B.C. V0N 1B4, tel: 604/938-8000, toll-free 1-800/606-8244, fax: 604/938-2020, <www.fairmont.com>.* Part of the Canadian Pacific Hotels group (which includes the Fairmont Hotel Vancouver, Waterfront Centre and the Empress), this ski and golf resort has won many travel industry awards. Elite, expensive and bursting with leisure amenities. Skiers should check out the low-season ski packages. Wheelchair accessible. 563 rooms.

Holiday Inn SunSpree Resort $$$$$ *4295 Blackcomb Way, Whistler, B.C. V0N 1B4, tel: 604/938-0878, toll-free 1-800/229-3188, (worldwide) 1-800/HOLIDAY, fax: 604/938-9943, <www.whistlerhi.com>.* This inn is a cross between a hotel and a condominium complex, and it will appeal both to skiers and to families taking a long holiday in Whistler. Studios and one- and two-bedroom suites include a fireplace and kitchen, although room service, of course, is only a phone call away, plus On Command movies, games and internet access. Some rooms have a den, loft or balcony. Bathrooms have luxurious tubs. Leisure amenities include a fitness centre and whirlpool. 115 rooms.

VANCOUVER ISLAND

Abigail's Hotel $$$$$ *906 McClure Street, Victoria, B.C. V8V 3E7, tel: 250/388-5363, toll-free 1-800/561-6565, fax: 250/388-7787, <www.abigailshotel.com>.* This Tudor-style inn, just three blocks away from the harbour, is a sanctuary for couples. The beautifully appointed rooms include private baths, and some also have fireplaces and Jacuzzi tubs. The service is comparable to that of a much larger hotel, but the atmosphere is much more intimate, and here guests have the added bonus of a hearty breakfast included in the rates. 23 rooms.

The Empress (Fairmont) $$$$$ *721 Government Street, Victoria B.C. V8W 1W5, tel: 250/384-8111, toll-free 1-800/441-1414, fax: 250/389-2747, <www.fairmont.com/empress>*. Once the beloved dowager of Victoria, where gloved and hatted ladies took tea amid brocade and antiques, this historic landmark hotel on the Inner Harbour remains the focal point of the city. A $50 million renovation in the late 1980s enlarged but somewhat depersonalised this icon, yet it still evokes a longing for civility, as evidenced by the 150,000 afternoon teas served here each year. Wheelchair accessible. 477 rooms.

James Bay Inn $$–$$$ *270 Government Street, Victoria, B.C. V8V 2L2, tel: 250/384-7151, toll-free 1-800/836-2649, fax: 250/385-2311, <www.jamesbayinn.com>*. The artist Emily Carr spent her last years at this pleasant inn with bay windows while it was a retirement home. Renovated in 1998, it's the third oldest operating hotel in the city and just four blocks from downtown. Budget-minded travellers will be pleased with the simple but tasteful rooms. Discounts for longer stays. 45 rooms.

Rosewood Victoria Inn $$–$$$$$ *595 Michigan Street, Victoria, B.C. V8V 1S7, tel: 250/384-6644, toll-free 1-800/335-3466, fax: 250/384-6117, <www.rosewoodvictoria.com>*. Two houses (one brand new) connected by an inner patio form this serene, three-storey decorator showcase that's a short walk from the harbour. Perfect for couples (children are discouraged), the large inviting rooms sport canopy beds, fireplaces and antiques; some have Jacuzzis. Gourmet breakfast included in the price. Wheelchair accessible. 17 suites.

Sooke Harbour House $$$$$ *1528 Whiffen Spit Road, Sooke, B.C. V0S 1N0, tel: 250/642-3421, toll-free, 1-800/889-9688, fax: 250/642-6988, <www.sookeharbourhouse.com>*. This romantic, secluded slice of paradise will remind you that life can indeed be extraordinary, from the fresh flowers to the original artwork displayed in every room. Rates include breakfast, to be enjoyed in front of your fireplace, on your balcony overlooking the ocean, or perhaps in bed. Wheelchair accessible. 28 rooms.

Recommended Restaurants

When a neighbourhood restaurant has a dozen customers waiting patiently on the pavement for a table on a rainy Monday night in November, you can be certain you've arrived in a town that enjoys its food. Don't waste a single meal while in Vancouver. The local ingredients are too tasty, the chefs are too passionate, and the energy is too enticing for you to end up in some tired concept restaurant with a menu specialising in boredom.

Along with the picks described below, find reliable dining recommendations in *City Foods* or in James Barber's *I Love Good Food Guide to Eating in Vancouver.* Your hotel's concierge is another source, but probably works from a patronage list. Do be sure to make dinner reservations which are essential in many places. Unless otherwise indicated, restaurants are open for lunch as well as dinner.

The price categories below indicate the approximate cost of a three-course meal, per person, excluding drinks, taxes (7 percent) and tips (15 percent), which will add considerably to your bill. Note that wine is especially expensive here due to high excise taxes.

$$$	Over $40
$$	$20–$40
$	under $20

DOWNTOWN

Allegro Café $$ *888 Nelson Street, tel: 604/683-8485.* Moderately priced Italian food in a spot the local cognoscenti have adopted. Notable soups, pastas and deftly prepared entrées. Don't let the upstairs location in an office building turn you off. Closed Sundays, closed for lunch on Saturdays.

Blue Water Café and Raw Bar $$$ *1095 Hamilton Street, tel: 604/688-8078.* Awards, for both food and wine, continue to keep pouring in to this excellent seafood restaurant in a funky converted warehouse in the heart of Yaletown. Appetisers, sushi, seafood on ice, entrées, oysters, desserts, cheese – all have separate (and lengthy) menus, so there's plenty of choice. The prix fixe menu, served 5–6pm, offers great value. Lunch not served.

C Restaurant $$$ *1600 Howe Street, (604) 681-1164.* Some folks are reluctant to order sea bass accompanied by gooseneck barnacles, but customers who stick around long enough to see if the kitchen is serious are in for a striking experience. This very sophisticated, innovative patio seafood restaurant on False Creek delivers food that is as beautiful and flavourful as it is unusual. The menu always includes something understandable for seafood lovers.

Diva at the Met $$$ *645 Howe Street, tel: 604/602-7788.* Elegant terraced room in the recently renovated Metropolitan Hotel, with an eclectic menu featuring seafood, modern North American cooking and great desserts. First-rate service, a stellar reputation and the use of what's seasonal keep Diva at the top of the 'Best of' lists. Stylish bar with food service in case you forgot to make a reservation. Open for breakfast.

Earl's on Top $ *1185 Robson Street, tel: 604/669-0020.* If you want a quick bite, any of the Earl's chain of restaurants are acceptable and easy places to eat, especially for families. Quality, imaginative food for the price, terrace dining available in summer.

Fleuri $$$ *Sutton Place Hotel, 845 Burrard Street, tel: 604/642-2900.* An exceptional hotel dining room. The surroundings are comfortable yet plush, a pianist plays standards in the background, and the Pacific Northwest menu is enticing and well-executed, featuring roasted rack of lamb with a lavender and grapefruit crust. Chocolate dessert buffet served Thursday through Saturday nights.

Hermitage $$$ *115–1025 Robson Street, tel: 604/689-3237.* Warm brick decor and French-influenced cooking combine to keep voices lowered and manners intact. Set in a courtyard off busy Robson, the patio is a quiet respite.

Hy's Encore $$$ *637 Hornby Street, tel: 604/683-7671.* This is the place to go for an old-fashioned char-grilled steak dinner with a Caesar salad constructed table-side, big baked potato and all the trimmings. It's a Vancouver tradition. Closed for lunch Saturdays and Sundays.

Il Giardino di Umberto $$$ *1382 Hornby Street, tel: 604/669-2422.* A table on the patio on a warm summer's day, something savoury from the outdoor brick oven, a glass of red wine, and your vacation has reached its peak. Inside, glance at the power lunchers dealing over fancy bowls of pasta. At night, savour the romance in one of the prettiest dining rooms outside Tuscany. Closed Sundays, lunch Saturdays.

Shanghai Chinese Bistro $ *1124 Alberni Street, tel: 604/683-8222.* Tasty Cantonese and Szechuan dishes are on offer here, featuring an extensive selection of fresh seafood and shellfish. Chefs make noodles from scratch in front of diners, and if you haven't ordered any, you'll wish you had. Great for *dim sum* at lunch. Located on the second floor of a nondescript building. Open until 1am weekends.

Yaletown Brewing Company $ *1111 Mainland Avenue, tel: 604/681-2739.* Brick walls and denim-covered banquettes define the casual atmosphere of this noisy (9 TVs), popular brew-pub on a Yaletown corner. Burgers, pasta, pizza and daily specials are prepared in an open kitchen in the main room and, of course, there's a large selection of house-brewed beers such as Frank's Nut Brown Ale and wheat beers on tap.

EAST OF DOWNTOWN

Havana $ *1212 Commercial Drive, tel: 604/253-9119.* The food, starting with breakfast and ending with dinner, has an Afro-Latino flavour, but may not be the main reason to make your way to the Grandview neighbourhood on the East Side. Consider your time here a funky cultural diversion. Sip excellent coffee, eat if you're hungry, and drink in the city as seen from one of its coolest districts.

Pink Pearl $ *1132 East Hastings Street, tel: 604/253-4316.* The din from business-lunchers, Chinese families and the *dim sum* carts rolling past the linen-covered tables creates the atmosphere in this cavernous, popular, award-winning Cantonese restaurant. Order from a lengthy menu, from the live seafood tank, or choose from a good variety of *dim sum*.

WEST END AND STANLEY PARK

Café de Paris $$ *751 Denman Street, tel: 604/687-1418.* The leek and duck confit tart here will have you speaking endearments to the chef, and you'll fight your friends over the greaseless, crispy *pommes frites* on the table. This very French bistro is a delight and a bargain at lunch, and you shouldn't miss it. Closed for lunch on Saturdays. Reservations essential.

Cardero's $$ *1583 Coal Harbour Quay, tel: 604/669-7666.* A spacious and casual restaurant with a menu that seeks to please a spectrum of tastes. Burgers, pizza and pasta should keep the kids calm, while the salads, the usual fish choices and gourmet steak dishes cover the needs of those with bigger appetites. The windows frame breathless North Vancouver and harbour views, and there's a great bar.

Fish House in Stanley Park $$ *8901 Stanley Park Drive, tel: 604/681-7275.* The location, by the English Bay entrance to the park, is a draw in itself. Speciality: tiger prawns sautéed with garlic, roasted red peppers, tomatoes and feta cheese, flambéed with ouzo, also classics such as an ahi tuna steak 'Diane', and a seductive fresh oyster bar.

Raincity Grill $$ *1193 Denman Street, tel: 604/685-7337.* The name celebrates Vancouver's famous precipitations; the food celebrates the first-class produce that comes from the local farmers and fishermen. This urban bistro across from English Bay has entrancing views, especially at sunset. The sophisticated Pacific Northwest cuisine features whatever's fresh, and the wine list is renowned. Portions are generous.

Sequoia Grill $$$ *7510 Stanley Park Drive (Ferguson Point), tel: 604/669-3281.* The garden-party surroundings, with mesmerising views of English Bay, are so warm and inviting that you want to make your meal last as long as possible. But that takes great self-control when faced with the seared beef salad or potato-crusted sea bass, or the eggs Benedict with bacon at brunch.

GRANVILLE ISLAND

Bridges $$ *1696 Duranleau Street, tel: 604/687-4400.* More terrific views, day and night. A $50 prix fixe dinner menu offers a wide variety of local delicacies with a seafood accent, and dessert. Bridges also features a dockside bistro wine bar for more casual (under $20) dining, outdoor dining and pub, as well as a popular Sunday brunch.

Dockside Brewing Company $$ *Granville Island Hotel, 1253 Johnston Street, tel: 604/685-7070.* A jaded young Vancouver businesswoman described this place as 'amazing', and she wasn't talking about the unique views of False Creek. The excellent menu touches on all the basics but leans towards seafood. There are also hand-crafted lagers and ales that taste even better when sipped on the patio accompanied by some grilled red curry prawns.

WEST SIDE

Bishop's $$$ *2183 West 4th Avenue, tel: 604/738-2025.* Bishop's remains at the pinnacle of the fine dining experience in Vancouver, with seasonal ingredients prepared simply and with the utmost regard for flavour. A special-occasion destination for the locals, and a must for gourmets.

Lumière $$$ *2551 West Broadway, tel: 604/739-8185.* Immerse yourself in the freshest, loveliest local ingredients combined by a much-celebrated local chef to excite the palate and please the eye. Order from the 'tasting menu' and settle in for a long, pleasurable evening. The modern setting is simple and comfortable. Open for dinner only, closed Monday.

Naam Restaurant $–$$ *2724 4th Avenue West, tel: 604/738-7151.* Frequently voted the best vegetarian restaurant in Vancouver, Naam has a 30-year history of serving natural food. Breakfasts are wonderful, and the lunch/dinner menu encompasses Mexican and Asian flavours. Live jazz, blues or folk music every night. Open 24 hours a day, every day except Christmas Day.

Provence Mediterranean Grill $$ *4473 West 10th Avenue, (604) 222-1980.* This Point Grey neighbourhood bistro fills with locals who appreciate the moderate prices and the tasty French (with a dollop of Italian) menu. Colourful, fresh antipasti make for a light starter, the crisp roasted chicken couldn't be better on a cold night. Hold out for a patio table at lunch on a sunny Vancouver day.

Sami's $ *986 West Broadway, tel: 604/736-8330.* Located in a tiny corner shopping centre, friendly Sami's serves tasty Indian food with a fusion twist. Dishes to investigate include tender beef short ribs in cumin and ginger, and a fragrant basmati rice paella. A genuine bargain, and the locals love it.

Season's Hill Top Bistro $$ *Queen Elizabeth Park, tel: 604/874-8008.* Perched on the highest point in the city, all the tables here take advantage of the panoramic views of Vancouver and beyond. The straightforward menu features fresh fish, proper salads, and desserts such as lemon pie.

Sophie's Cosmic Café $ *2095 West 4th Avenue, tel: 604/732-6180.* Eclectic and hip and a particularly smart choice for families. You can order a delicious breakfast that will keep you going almost until dinner, which Sophie's also serves. The wait at weekends can be long, with the queue starting at 9am.

Tojo's $$$ *202-777 West Broadway, Suite 202, tel: 604/872-8050.* This dignified, innovative Japanese restaurant is reputed to have the best sushi to be found anywhere. Take a seat at the bar and let Tojo himself take your order. He's an innovative sushi artist, but if this is not your dish of saki, repair to the elegant tatami room, where you sit Japanese-style on cushions.

Vij's $$ *1480 West 11th Avenue, tel: 604/736-6664.* Diners wait patiently outside, knowing nothing is worth the wait as much as dinner at this innovative Indian bistro where the menu changes monthly. Very highly recommended. Friendly service, ethereal atmosphere. The home-made sparkling ginger lemon drink is a treat. Open for dinner only. No reservations.

WEST VANCOUVER

The Beach House at Dundarave Pier $$$ *150 25th Street, West Vancouver, tel: 604/922-1414.* The heated oceanfront patio is but one of three dining levels from which to view magnificent Burrard Inlet at this elegant restaurant. Fresh main ingredients are presented with unusual flair, with accents such as basil red pepper crème and rosemary goat cheese. A tower of three cheesecakes dominates the desserts.

Beach Side Café $$ *1362 Marine Drive, West Vancouver, tel: 604/925-1945.* This is a wonderful location with a picture-postcard view of Vancouver's West Side. The bonus is a West Coast menu prepared with an experienced, deft hand. It's the kind of neighbourhood restaurant that makes you fervently wish you lived around the corner.

WHISTLER

Araxi $$$ *4222 Whistler Village Square, tel: 604/932-4540.* Araxi's relaxed dining room and its versatile indoor-outdoor bar anchors the resort's lively patio scene. The emphasis here is on fresh, locally sourced food, ranging from Gulf Islands smoked albacore tuna brochettes with organic peach salsa, minted cucumber, tobiko and cilantro syrup, to Lillooet honey crème brûlée. Lunch seasonal.

Val d'Isère $$$ *4314 Main Street, tel: 604/932-4666.* Superchef Roland Pfaff presides over the kitchen here, offering palate-pleasing delicacies from the Alcase region, such as a signature onion tart. The Queen Charlotte Islands smoked herring and Granny

Smith apple salad, served in a buttery potato mille-feuille with smoked-mussel vinaigrette, are heartwarming, and desserts are cameo works of art.

BOWEN ISLAND

Blue Eyed Mary's $–$$ *433 Trunk Road, tel: 604/947-0550.* For a memorable evening, take the ferry from Horseshoe bay to Bowen Island and walk up the main street to this cosy spot. The seasonal west coast themed menu, with French and Italian influences, changes monthly. Reservations are a must. Closed Monday and Tuesday. Lunch not served.

VANCOUVER ISLAND

Café Brio $$ *944 Fort Street, Victoria, tel: 250/383-0009, toll-free 1-866/270-5461.* A few blocks from downtown in a handsome wrought-iron trimmed stucco house. Organically grown produce and fresh local ingredients combine to create a seasonally changing contemporary West Coast menu. Lively ambiance. Open for dinner only.

Marina Restaurant $$$ *1327 Beach Drive, Victoria, tel: 250/598-8555.* Victoria's best seafood restaurant is set, as the name suggests, right on the edge of the Marina in the classy Oak Bay suburb, with plenty of windows to maximise the view. West Coast and Japanese cuisines combine to provide an interesting menu that ranges from traditional chowders to sushi to grilled ahi tuna, plus some first-rate meat dishes. Light lunches are also available, plus a memorable Sunday brunch – and great cocktails, too.

Sooke Harbour House $$$ *1528 Whiffen Spit Road, Sooke, tel: 250/642-3421.* The restaurant at this beautiful inn is a destination in itself. Once named by *The Globe and Mail* as Canada's best restaurant, it has also been listed as one of the world's top spots. Meals here use vegetables, fruits and berries that are grown at the inn, plus local fish, meat from Island producers and other foraged items. Open for dinner only.

INDEX

Accommodation 104–5, 126–34
Ambleside Park 60
Arts Club Theatre 43

Barclay Square Heritage Park 32
B.C. Place Stadium 44
B.C. Sports Hall of Fame 44
Blackcomb Mountain 63, 65
Bloedel Conservatory 52–3
Bowen Island 61–2
Crippen Regional Park 61
Snug Cove 61
Butchart Gardens 74–5
Butterfly Gardens 75

Canada Place 26, 34
Capilano Park and Suspension
    Bridge 55, 59
Cathedral Place 37
Centre in Vancouver for the
    Performing Arts 37
Chan Centre for the Performing
    Arts 49–50
children 90–92
Children's Farmyard 29
Chinatown 26, 40–1
Chinese Cultural Centre 41
Christ Church Cathedral 37
Commercial Drive 25, 53–4

Denman Street 33
Dr Sun Yat-Sen Classical Garden
    41

Eating out 94–102, 135–42
East Side 53–4

English Bay 25
entertainment and nightlife 77–82

Fairmont Hotel Vancouver 37
False Creek 26, 42
festivals and special events 93

Gastown 38–9
Granville Bridge 42
Granville Island 26, 42–3
Granville Island
    Public Market 43
Grouse Mountain 50, 58
Grouse Mountain Skyride 58

Hastings Mill Store 48
history 13–23
Hiwus Feathouse 50
Horseshoe Bay 60–1
Howe Sound 60, 62
H.R. MacMillan Space Centre 47

Ironworkers' Memorial
    (Second Narrows) Bridge 55

Jericho Beach Park 48
Junior Creek hatchery 58

Kids Only Market 43
Kitsilano 25, 26, 45–8
Kitsilano Beach Park 48
Koerner Ceramics Gallery 51

Library Square 36–7
Little Italy 53–4
Lonsdale Quay 55–6

Lost Lagoon 31
Lower Seymour Conservation
  Reserve 57
Lynn Canyon Park 56

Malkin Bowl 31
Marine Building 38
Miniature Railway 29
Mount Seymour Park 55
Museum of Anthropology 50–1

Nat Bailey Stadium 53
Nature House 31
Nitobe Memorial Garden 51
North Vancouver 54–9

Pacific Spirit Regional Park 49
Park Royal 60
Pioneer Park 48
Point Atkinson Lighthouse 60
Point Grey 49
Prospect Point 29–30

Queen Elizabeth Park 52–3

Refuge for Endangered Wildlife 58
Rice Lake 57–8
Robson Square 35–6
Robson Street 35–7
Roedde House Museum 32–3

Sam Kee Building 41
Science World 44
Sea to Sky Highway 64–5
Second Beach 31
Seymour Falls Dam 57
Shannon Falls 65
shopping 82–5

Silk Road 40
Sinclair Centre 35
Sooke 75
South Granville 25
sports 86–9
Squamish 62
Stanley Park 26, 27–31
Steam Clock 39
Steveston 66–8
Storyeum 39

TELUSphere 44
Theatre Under the Stars 31
transport 35, 43, 68–9

University of B.C. 49–51
U.B.C. Botanical Gardens 52

Vancouver Aquarium Marine
  Science Centre 31
Vancouver Art Gallery 36
Vancouver Folk Festival 48
Vancouver Island 68–75
Vancouver Maritime Museum 47
Vancouver Museum 46–7
VanDusen Botanical Garden 52
Vanier Park 46–7
Victoria 69–74

Waterfront Station 34–5
West End 26, 32–3
West Side 45–53
West Vancouver 60–1
Whistler 63–6
World Famous Lumberjack
  Show 58

Yaletown 26, 44